THE TRIADIC SINGULARITY

Humanity's Final Frontier
For Transforming Earth Into Heaven

KEVIN ZEPH

Dedicated to all those seeking peace.

PREFACE

Welcome, this is your formal introduction to the Triadic Singularity.

The Triadic Singular is a systematic approach for simplifying and mentally structuring some of the more complex cycles of human karma. This system has not been set forth to marginalize the intricacies of each person's uniquely difficult predicament, in fact this approach of systematization has been sculpted with quite the opposite intent of bringing heightened clarity and renewed confidence into the hearts and minds of each being whose eyes are meant to read these words.

As you come to understand each of the societal singularities, their coalescence into the Triadic Singularity, and the implications of how to live your own life in alignment with the potential of cultivating a golden era on Earth, the value of this system will be self evident.

The more clearly you can see the vision of what an enlightened society would really look like, and what an enlightened version of yourself would act like, the easier it will be to step into the ultimate version of our potential to be instrumental figures for transformation.

Wherever you are on the journey through life, I hope this book serves your understanding through its exploration of societal cycles.

May humanity flourish into a completely realized manifestation of its peaceful and prolific potential.

May all beings live's be overflowingly filled with nothing but bliss.

Thank you for joining me in the priceless contemplation of the Triadic Singularity, may it swiftly come to fruition for the benefit of all sentient beings.

With Love,
Kevin Zeph

PART ONE:

THE TRIAD

1: THE STATE OF AFFAIRS

Our planet is in absolute peril.

Look around.

What is the state of affairs on planet Earth according to your personal assessment?

It seems undeniable that we have found ourselves in some truly turbulent times. Human history has been filled with a near unending succession of war. So many revolutions have occurred. So many reformations have occurred. So many leaders have come and gone, each with clear plans and passionate followings, but to what avail?

The environmental conditions of our planet are at their worst in recorded history while the average person is in a constant state of psychological tension. When we earnestly investigate the conditions in which humanity is collectively living, it appears dreadfully fragile at best. There doesn't seem to be a clear and stable outcome approaching on the horizon any time soon.

Although human suffering has unflinchingly remained throughout our evolutionary history, societal difficulties seem to occur cyclically. Empires rise and empires fall. Peace treaties are made and then they are broken. Religions promote peace and then they often become the center of so much conflict. Breakthroughs of innovation are made which seem to better people's lives and then they are exploited by the highest bidder, furthering the divide between the powerful and powerless. Thanks to planned obsolescence, this week's innovation becomes next week's landfill pile.

Our smartphones feed our inner tensions through a culture of sound bites. Social media was literally constructed to be as addictive as a slot machine that we all keep conveniently tucked away in our pockets. Meanwhile, we are fed with a constant stream of out-groups to hate and in-groups to self validate. The degradation of humanity's collective mental health has been manufactured. Agitation and dis-ease have become the most prevalent first-world diseases. Technology is supposed to bring us into greater heights of life, but our misuse has led to a communicative breakdown and a sense of separation from the people who are actually near us. We have been collectively reared into unparalleled tension and unparalleled anger. Meanwhile, there are numerous genocides and famines scattering the globe, conveniently made to be nearly invisible by the mainstream media.

Humanity's population keeps rising despite scientific indications of overpopulation. The density of human existence is now giving rise to all sorts of unexpected problems, such as the global pandemic of 2020. The quality of life slowly is decaying for everyone except those who continue to profit off of our collective demise. Most of the food made available is so cheaply made that even citizens of the modernized world remain malnourished. The culture of ultra-processed foods has stripped our collective wellness.

Systemic racism continues to be a dominant theme in America and every nation whose roots were grown in imperialism. White privilege has compounded its manipulative tactics to the point where there is no longer a clear path for untangling the web of its influence that has distorted every sector of our economy and culture. The privatized prison system and for-profit probationary structures are just slavery's next evolutionary stages in an unbroken procession of subversion. Slavery is alive and well, albeit in a subliminal state.

Now the constitutional right of peaceful protesting and authentic journalism are being suppressed by a wave of accepted police brutality. It seems that the intelligent agencies puppeteering the powers that be are trying to make a peaceful revolution impossible to achieve. As a result, the more violent acts of looting and physical retaliation seem to many like the only possible approaches left for seeking change. Since violence is an easily demonizable and dismissible approach, the justifiable call of the revolutionary's heart yearning for change has so few remaining outlets to help our broken world that justice is starting to feel like an unattainable pipe dream.

No one is fully equipped to manage our society as we move forward in a world of fake news and half-truth. Our egos have been manipulated by villainous and greedy individuals hiding behind impenetrable curtains. We are facing unprecedented levels of joblessness, homelessness, and hopelessness. The cycles of suffering keep circling around and around.

Unless meaningful reform is constructed on behalf of those who suffer, there will always be an inevitably subsequent uprising by the oppressed. The cycle of degradation and revolution will continue so long as justice hasn't become the status quo for policymaking. If the language of the prophets is to be applied in the depiction of the planet's actual state of affairs, it wouldn't be too far fetched to label this the era of darkness or the age of demons.

Currently, chaos prevails. A lot of people would prefer to trudge through the misery of life, and witness many suffer, rather than figure out how to peacefully bring order to this broken realm. Luckily for us, the number of good-hearted and compassionate people on the planet far outnumber the ones only interested in personal gain. Unfortunately, those who push and shove for personal gain and power are usually the ones with the most influence and control. Those whose inner drive and ego empower them to gain dominance in our ill-constructed society become kings and leaders among us. Those same egos are the ones making the laws that bind us to the turbulences resulting from greed and entrap us to patterns of activities that are motivated by the self-interest of a few individuals.

Somehow, someway, we have to establish harmony and prevailing compassion throughout the world during this intensely complicated new age of global interrelation.

But how?

2: THE PILLARS

There are so many factors creating the sense of unsolvable chaos in our world and lives. It is hard to even keep track of the numerous problems at hand, let alone conceive of viable solutions that simultaneously work for each situation without inadvertently creating more complications in the process. One never knows which approach will truly be the best for the collective well being. The wedding planner prays for sun while the farmer prays for rain.

Many people have ideas for solving the entanglements facing humanity that they view are most pressing; however, there don't seem to be many comprehensive approaches or clear plans as to how we might manage all of the variables comprising each of the myriad of problems at hand simultaneously. The problems have become so overgrown that many people feel that, environmentally and politically, a long-term global stability is beyond humanity's collective grasp. It may appear as if there is no end to the chaos in sight and that there is no hope of bringing our world into an era of total peace.

To really address these difficulties we are going to have to take a step back. To establish a clear view of the interconnected entanglements at play and understand the origins of our difficulties, we must first delineate the processes in motion. The problems are numerous, but their sources are few. To start, it is easy to see that the majority of the difficulties at hand are human difficulties and therefore the majority of the solutions will also have to be human solutions.

We could easily sit here all day and count the problems towering over the future of mankind without ever reaching the bottom of the list. Instead, let us assess the arenas of human influence, which are currently causing us conflict, in a more categorical manner. By methodically organizing the strings of difficulties, we will much more easily be able to untangle the web of difficulties we have woven around ourselves.

All of society's problems can be boiled down into essential categories. Each category has its own natural cycles which are determined by humanity's collective patterns of activity relative to these individual spheres. These categories are the pillars of human influence which are at play in our the current state of disarray. To uncover the categories of society we must dissect what it is that makes us evolutionarily unique as humans and therefore what defines human civilization as a whole.

For one, our sense of community is so engrained and complex that we have orchestrated and organized human interaction on a larger and more detailed scale than any other species in Earth's known history. The organization of human interaction is essential to the formation of civilization and therefore what can loosely be called politics is undeniably one of the core pillars needing investigation as we uncover the patterns caused by human influence.

We as humans, quite noticeably, also have the unique capacity to conceive of more advanced concepts and to use our intellects to construct more intricate mechanisms than any other known species on Earth. The use of tools has always been fundamental to the human identity and the formation of civilization; therefore, technology is also one of the basic pillars constituting societal formation.

Finally, humans have such a uniquely introspective nature that we are able to reflect on our relationship to the whole of phenomena more so than any other known species on the planet. Self-belief, identity, culture, and philosophy are completely fundamental to what defines the human experience and to the formation of human civilization. The systemization of belief, which may be generalized as religion, is the third essential pillar of society.

The three pillars which are essential to our species' construction of civilization and their corresponding arenas of definable influence, which are inherently worth investigating during the contemplation of how to cultivate harmony on Earth, can be labeled simply as politics, technology, and religion. The three things you're never supposed to bring up at a dinner party are the three things that unavoidably require unyielding analysis, if humanity is ever to determine a proper path to collective wellbeing that is.

These are the three pillars.

Each of these categorical pillars has its own pattern of growth and decay. Each of the pillars naturally undergoes its own evolution and series of cycles respective to humanity's development over the course of societal history. These categories of society and human influence have had their ups and downs, their positive progressions and their crippling impact to the planet and its people throughout the myriad of different phases.

With all of the globally problematic situations currently at hand, it seems like each of these categories is at a point of simultaneous critical capacity. Will the three pillars soon crumble? Or will we be able to break our destructive patterns, as to slowly stabilize society's operation, effectively saving our species and planet?

If so, when? And how?

Each of the pillars must reach their own state of harmony and stasis during this globalized stage of the project of humanity, if we wish to continue existing as a species into the unforeseeable future. The point where the globally interconnected sectors of society become truly mutually stable can be deemed as the point Triadic Singularity.

You may be familiar with the term Technological Singularity. This refers to the point at which our technological achievement is in such a state that artificial intelligence technology can produce its own self-generated advancement at such an exponential rate that it functions without human influence and therefore at a rate beyond the capacity of development ever possible for humans thus far.

In regard to the Triadic Singularity, this notion of a singularity point will be investigated as it relates to the three societal pillars. On an abstract level, it is important to understand the notion of a singularity before it is applied to each of the three pillars or interwoven into a vision of these three singularities reaching a collective point of synthesis.

As the culmination of the singularities of each of the three pillars unfolds, they will inherently merge into what can be deemed the Triadic Singularity. The singularity of these singularities is the gateway to living in an enlightened society. Exponentially positive growth of the three primary spheres, or pillars, of society is required for humanity to remain on Earth despite the obstacles ahead. This level of self-synchronic functioning can be known as living in an enlightened society, which is the point at which Triadic Singularity is embodied. The three pillars meet, forming a pyramid.

The Triadic Singularity is only achieved when the three primary facets of human civilization are functioning as one harmonious super-organism, of sorts, which is a perpetually stable society on Earth. Thus, the Triadic Singularity will inevitably be born within humanity as the cycles of systems coalesce, if we are able to maintain our species' existence through the trials of the age of globalization, that is.

If not, we are doomed to slide back into the times of tribal warfare, perhaps continued nationalistic disharmony, or maybe even become extinct entirely.

3: SURE WAY

We have come incredibly far in our species' endeavor towards collective human progress. Our project of societal development has flourished in so many exquisite ways. It would be such an unbearable shame to lose generations of efforts on our quest to maintaining a stabile and globally interconnected society. Yet, we are teetering on the edge of destruction at the hands of our own ignorance, greed, and lust for life. Our blind pursuit of self-indulgence has led us to the precipice of collapse. It is not clear whether we will collectively pull through these current conditions or not. As our progress intensifies, so has the tenuousness of our fate. We have reached a height of development, but at what cost? The quality of life has increased for many and yet remains completely turbulent and tumultuous for so many more, including the literal planet's environmental health. In the era of globalization, we have come very close to rectifying the blood-soaked path that we marched to reach this point, but still we somehow continue to be pulled back into more wars and escalating disenfranchisement of many races and nations comprising our beautiful, one-world family.

We have failed to close the cyclical loops of self-inflicted human despair time and time again. If we are going to become participants in a globally harmonious civilization, we must achieve systematic unity within the societal pillars that have continually reinforced our destructive patterns: politics, technology, and religion.

Our unavoidable quest to master the construction of each of these systems will either lift us up into global sustainability or drag us down into further oppressive patterns of cyclical suffering.

The Triadic Singularity is the only sure way.

Without reaching the point of sustainable, self-regulated function within the spheres of society's categories, disparity will continue to haunt us and eventually take the reins of our collective fate. We have seen this unfortunate outcome so many times over in human history already. So many advanced empires have come and gone, slain by the hands of the next soon to fail leaders in line. We must without a doubt find peace within our political relations, sustainability within our use of technology, and mutual acceptance within our religious functionings, or else we are doomed to countless more years of debate and subsequent warring amongst our species' population.

We have reached the edge of the cliff. There is no turning back without unbearable tragedy and there is no way forward without working with the conditions at hand. We have begun the project of globalization and there is no easy way around its complicated implications. We absolutely must develop mutually beneficial systems for all sentient beings or else we will surely bomb ourselves back into another era of pre-history.

If we do not make the project of globalization beneficial for every single group of people, there will surely be uprising after uprising and rebellion after rebellion until our unavoidable decay leads into a new tribal era. Unless we find symbiosis amongst all human factions, we are bound to increase our division again over time.

There is nothing wrong with a world filled with tiny communities. A society reduced to renewed tribalism would certainly prevent any further nuclear warfare in the near future. The tribalistic lifestyle certainly has some advantages. Perhaps that is the most our species can handle. If we can't play nicely with our toys, we probably shouldn't have them at all.

That being said, there has been so much bloodshed to reach this point in our societal progression, it seems dreadfully unfortunate to imagine losing this opportunity to achieve world peace. Not to mention the fact that any new regimes of this hypothetical future with a fractured society will also pine and fight for power until they too slowly absorb tribe after tribe and eventually become another iteration of human imperialism which sits in our very same fork in the very same road of collective fate. The egoic lust for power keeps the societal wheel turning. If we fail we will once again start the movement through tribalism, feudalism, nationalism, and quickly circle back to globalism.

This has actually happened time and time again throughout history. Eventually, a few dominant tribes become the new nations and lead us right back into the predicament of seeking peaceful globalization. The slow evolution from tribalism into nationalism is not possible without unspeakable chaos and horrific amounts of bloodshed.

The process releases hell onto our Earth. I don't wish that amount of suffering on my worst enemies, let alone the good natured majority of those who live and those who are to come.

These are the two paths before us: harmonize on a global scale or revert to the cyclical struggles which have plagued the fractured existences comprising the previous versions of human civilizations.

The path to harmony isn't clear, but attaining the Triadic Singularity is the only sure way to not only avoid another hellish era on Earth but also to finally exist in an era where the Earth can reach a Heaven-like state of global well being.

4: POLITICAL SINGULARITY

What a journey we are on.

Our connectivity and development of complex communicative systems eventually gave humanity the evolutionary edge needed to become dominantly established in each of the world's respective regions. Our evolutionary advantage became so powerful that we stumbled all the way through our primitive habits until we formulated full-fledged civilizations. Our tribalistic organization was an organic expansion of the uniquely intelligent capacities we hold as a species. The same natural progression led us to another new and uncharted territory of our evolution as a species on Earth: the project of consciously constructing systems of self-governance.

Our tribes became villages, our villages became towns, our towns became cities. Our cities turned into nation-states and now after thousands of years of meticulous organization and continual struggles between various factions for temporary dominance, we have reached the stage of globalization.

Our current line-up of empires and political factions are merely extensions of the evolutionary journey; from all the way back to the days of single-celled organisms striving to become bacteria through becoming the myriad of more complex organisms: all of our developments individually and societally are connected through the spectrum of events comprising material evolution. Up until the last few hundred years, our conflicts have been relatively tempered, vaguely akin to animals in a tussle or a group of kids fighting over a ball. Unfortunately, our chess matches have been invested in to a level beyond feasible belief. We have undergone an extremely slow arc leading to the multi-trillion dollar military industrial complex fueled clash of Empires who are battling it out to establish control over who determines humanity's collective rearing.

As long as we continue with this mentality of individualism and self-preservation over collective well-being, we will be digging the graves of all our future generations. Until the needs of all communities are authentically honored by the lawmakers, empires will continue to rise and fall. If the people are forced to speak on their own behalf, they will do so through any means possible: be it protest or destructive uprising.

The systems of control are supposed to be designed for the benefit of the people. If the powers that be hope to keep their position without ushering in another era of revolt than they are going to have to construct a system which benefits the masses, not just the rich. The heightening interconnectedness between all people on a international scale is an obviously unavoidable factor as we continue to develop in the era of globalization.

As a result, the ever-increasing singularization of humanity's collective fate is inevitable. All our activity is linked and the repercussions of our actions will also always be mutually destined. Without emphasizing a universally compassionate structure of political governance, the discord and cycles of corresponding revolution from the oppressed will always lurk in the not too distant, shadowy corners of our own apathy.

The historical progression of power-struggles has led to those in control institutionalizing their dominance which has compounded privilege and disenfranchised the many. This process has developed in such an incestuous manner that even the middle class has been squeezed into near oblivion, leaving most of the human population in a struggle to make ends meet while the fat cats sit back and delight in the design of their rat race.

The exact system we develop doesn't actually matter, just as long as it is rooted in compassion. We needn't develop a system with equal outcome, but we must at least strive to develop a system with equal opportunity and a basic dignity of lifestyle provided for all. Meeting each individual's basic, survival needs as a birthright won't eliminate the opportunity for those with capitalistic motivation to still acquire more wealth, it merely means there will be a safety net to eliminate the worst of humanity's suffering. This is the only way to avoid the cycles of corresponding revolution which have plagued human history thus far.

The need for ethical governance is paramount for political stabilization. Our leaders must be held accountable for acting fundamentally compassionate. We don't need a one-world government to be unified in global cooperation. That's all that is meant by the term "Political Singularity". The Political Singularity is nothing more than the point at which the sub-systems of human organization work together in actually serving the goodwill of the people.

There are many ways to approach the Political Singularity and each sub-division of government doesn't necessarily have to follow the same template to achieve world peace. Political Singularity doesn't imply a one-world government, but it does imply a world whose political systems unified in the attempt of actually striving for harmony. There are infinite viable variations of the Political Singularity which can be implemented with authentic effort towards humanity's systematization of harmony, but compassion will always be the fundamentally key ingredient.

As we exist in a world of interconnected global politics, we must learn to function in a world of interconnected global politics. This is the only meaning of the phrase Political Singularity.

Our political construction is meant to serve the needs of the people and until that is its primary function, we are doomed to breed more cycles of chaos and suffering for everyone in the web of human experience.

An easy way to conceive of a functional Political Singularity would be to work backward from your own personal political ideal to where we are now and slowly envision the work required to bridge that gap with new policies and approaches that are brimming with conscience and compassion.

Have you ever attempted to imagine a futuristic political system which could actually function on a global scale?

Does it look anything like the way our world functions today?

Does your vision for our collective ideal future consist of homelessness? What about people who have to choose between paying for health care and groceries?

Probably not.

If you take a moment to contemplate such a harmonious potential for society, how do you *really* envision its configuration? These musings are absolutely essential if we hope to reach the creative solutions needed to deal with the global issues at hand.

The task of achieving Political Singularity is no small feat. This singularity of politics is not about submitting to an Illuminati type "Big Brother" or even becoming uniformly submissive to one world view, let alone system of governance.

What the Political Singularity is truly about is humbly working together towards a brighter future in which all people can live with the dignity of their basic needs being met. We must learn to love and care for each culture and country as much as we care about our own.

It won't be the easiest of tasks but it must be achieved or else we are certainly all doomed to repeating the cycles of revolt and chaos that have plagued the previous empires throughout the history of human life on Earth.

5: TECHNOLOGICAL SINGULARITY

Humanity's slow and arduous development has involved so many stages leading to this point. From the days of tree-dwelling and forest living, we inched our way out into the fields. We have gone from gripping tree limbs and warding off tigers with sticks and rocks to now cultivating weapons of increasing intellectual design, capable of destroying life on Earth as we know it.

One of the most fundamental factors of human evolution is the co-dependent nature of our journey with technological innovations. The quality of human living and, to some degree, the quality of human consciousness has been linked to the inventions we utilize as we orient our daily existences. Over the years, humans have organically exercised our intellects to stretch and meet the evolving needs of a changing world and its constant pressures. Having opposable thumbs and consciousnesses bent on utilizing our ability to grip with our hands has been a driving force in establishing our leg up on the threats to survival. Initially, this use of technology was directed solely towards overcoming the elements and other species, but in time we have essentially conquered these basic pressures.

Our ability to create more and more protective places of dwelling, as well as weapons of greater capacity has led us to a place of supposed prominence over the rest of the food chain. Some of humanity's most historically profound paradigm shifts were nexus points derived from a revolution of technology. Be it the development of using metals for farming and machinery, the use of combustion to revolutionize war or travel, the development of electricity to animate our mechanisms and enhance our communication: there have been numerous eras of history which were spawned by advancing technologically. All of these inventions were sparked by fulfilling some want or need of our species to a deeper degree, until recently. At a certain point, our maniacal fixation upon advancing our weapons technology was no longer needed to establish stability within our environment.

We have reached a point now where the use and development of technology have left us almost completely disconnected from one another and ourselves. The technological arc of developmental intent moved from establishing a higher quality of human experience into the arena of solely fueling our blind pursuit of distraction from discomfort at all costs.

From the time of the industrial revolution, we have been hellbent on manufacturing as many products as the beast of consumptive desires could manage to digest. Likewise, we have continued this chase into the age of planned obsolescence and even into the age of seeking to establish life on other planets without any clear sense of its necessity, let alone sustainability.

In fact, we are tirelessly pursuing these dramatic technological goals despite their clearly over-consumptive costs. Meanwhile, our planet withers before our eyes. Still, our pursuit of ever-increasing technological enhancement continues. We are caught in an unsustainable loop of invention and production due to greedy individual pursuits without regard for environmental repercussions.

The sphere of artificially intelligent technology has brought us nearer and nearer to the point known as Technological Singularity. Technological Singularity has become a popular phrase in our society. The idea is that artificial intelligence will reach such a point of advancement that it will be able to create and learn at an exponentially increasing and self-regulated rate. At the singularity point, the result of human invention will be so complex that the technology itself will intelligently evolve faster than will ever be possible through collective human effort. Imagine a system of Artificially Intelligent computers that can instantly communicate to one another and are each processing faster than the human brain will ever be capable of. This degree of computation could easily get beyond the reaches of human management, like a child whose autonomy has developed beyond the limits willed by its parents. At this point, it is theorized that there will be the potential for complete biological and technological symbiosis.

The phrase Technological Singularity has always been the call sign for trans-humanism and the notion of some sort of Android-esque species which will become the new dominant life form of Earth.

While the interconnected technological development continues to peak and grow from mutual conclusions reached by the network of collective artificial intelligence, the intellectual thresholds of humanity will be continually broken every moment. Whether this involves physical symbiosis with AI or not, amazing feats will be achieved and profound inventions will be birthed. This will indeed be an era requiring tremendous humility in regards to the human conceit of perceived inherent-dominance.

So long as mankind is still able to directly control this exponentially increasing intelligence, humanity will be able to utilize AI to fulfill its many goals. However, at what point will the autonomy and agenda of this Artificial Intelligence outweigh the will of the humans which spawned this computerized intelligence in the first place? Just like the birth of free will within the evolution of biological species, technology may have a moment where its own independent ego structure develops free will. Countless science fiction thinkers have meticulously explored the dystopian potential lying down the path where artificial intelligence takes the reins of our collective human fate.

Although, it is worth noting that the true Technological Singularity is beyond our current understanding, by definition. Perhaps it has very little to do with AI. Yet, we have already entered into a grey area of trans-humanism in ways that are far less obvious than most realize. The constant use of smart phones is akin to our species having some sort of detached computational-implant. Anything you want to know, any person you wish to contact, and nearly any action you wish to execute are often only as far as away from us as a few types and swipes. In this way we may be considered a population of androids already.

Few people likely predicted the scientific design of the modern vaccination technology which was designed to alter our mRNA's coding much like we program a computer. Is this already the era of combining human biology with technology in an android-like fashion? It is difficult to say with certainty, but the implication is clear: the presentation of trans-humanism and the reality of what a Technological Singularity would even look like is yet to be revealed. It is a revolution of unforeseeable innovation by definition. The other clear reflection of our use of technology thus far is that we haven't been using the gift of abundance within reasonable sustainability.

Without a clearly directive ethic guiding our era of mass production, where do we really believe the roller coaster of invention is leading? Conscientiousness must be more fundamentally interwoven into our efforts of technological advancement if we wish to continue our existence on this planet, let alone any other.

We have to clearly envision our ideal regarding the use of technology and the appropriately balanced lifestyle of its production in accordance with the limits of the Earth. This doesn't mean we must retreat to primitivism or end the age of invention, but it does mean this exploration must be held within the limits of our resources.

We can still work toward reaching interplanetary habitation if we want to. This process must simply be harnessed into the arena of sustainability over profitability. The rate at which we are burning fossil fuels can only take us so far in our race to traverse the cosmos.

We must focus on our ability to invent alternative fuel systems, harnessing the abundance of energy that is freely floating in the universe. Eventually, we will be able to reverse engineer technology that can help us explore the vastness of space such as anti-gravity or time-space defying systems of travel. Perhaps we will reach a point of technological advancement which will allow us to dip in and out of the physical space-time grid, allowing travel at the speed of light or even thought.

The potential of futuristic manifestations aside, our basic use of daily products worldwide has yet to find sustainability. The possibilities are endless, but only as long as we don't derail our efforts at the hand of our own crippling greed.

It doesn't actually matter how technology is revolutionized, so many alternatives of sustainability can assist us on this journey. For example, by embracing the use of hemp we could decrease our negative impact on the planet with immense ease. Hemp has a 12-to-1 more effective yield ratio compared to that of trees. We could create paper, fuel, and even houses out of products utilizing hemp, but we don't due to lobbyists' influence over lawmakers.

The same is true with the transition from fossil fuels to green technologies such as solar and wind power. As long as greed is the dominant factor guiding our progression technologically, we are doomed in so many regards. We must take the power out of the hands of those with their minds on their pockets and into the hands of those with the entirety of the planet and its inhabitants in mind. Our use of technology must be aligned with the economy secondarily and with the collective needs of humanity primarily. As a result of our materialistic approach, so many people's entire lives have tragically become cog-like in the machine of societal desire. This is the truest failure of our time and people.

We have lost focus on the essence of technology which is to uplift the human experience. We absolutely must re-engineer our development and use of technology to properly continue on the path of human evolution.

The Technological Singularity is not about all, reducing the complex human condition to a single need, or becoming a hybrid symbiote of man and machine; However, the Technological Singularity is about reaching a harmonious point where technology is serving humanity's betterment sustainably. This should be the goal of all technological progression.

A lot of esteemed thinkers speak with absolute certainty about what the Technological Singularity will look like, how it will occur, and even when it will occur. They all presume that it will be achieved through this inherently linear path of humans developing artificial intelligence until the inventions become their own inventors. In reality, we do not know what the Technological Singularity will look like, how it will happen, or when it will happen.

If we did, we would already be living it.

We don't know if the Technological Singularity will actually occur from some impending communication of innovations with a race of intelligently advanced beings. Maybe it is the point where we actually merge societies with a race of aliens or become our own iteration of an interplanetary society through the integration of artificial and biological innovations like neural implants.

If we actually breach the realm of developing autonomous artificial intelligence, we must be careful that we are not merely inventing our replacement species but instead creating our most beneficial asset for an increased quality of human experience.

The line is fine, but with compassion and sustainability as our guides, we will naturally find our way to navigating these unfamiliar territories as the Technological Singular is inevitably born.

6: RELIGIOUS SINGULARITY

Is space truly the final frontier? Or perhaps there are realms to traverse beyond the physical. Throughout humanity's evolution, the search for deeper meaning and the mysterious secrets hidden within phenomena has always played a prominent role in our collective identity. It seems that as long as human civilization has existed there have also been systems of belief in place that define humanity's role in the cosmos.

Seeking and attempting to define the truth is fundamental to the human condition. Every civilization, regardless of geographic location, has cultivated its own mystic heritage, or pseudo-religion, relative to its people. In fact, the religious identity is such a centralized face of any particular culture that can be viewed as a primary pillar that invariably guides the patterns determining societal development as a whole. All religions are already one and have always been in singularity despite their appearances being so disparate as they are all attempts to define the undefinable relative to the culture and time in which they developed.

Religious traditions are united at the core level of being descriptive systems for the bigger picture, but they have each gone through many varying cycles of appearance.

Each of these cycles begins from the same point: an authentic mystic has experiences that give them deep insight into the nature of phenomena beyond what the limited minds of the masses are capable of understanding. As the prophet which originated each religious tradition pass their knowledge along to those around them, the truth naturally gets distorted into language-based belief systems. Slowly, these systems of belief become formalized into religions to maintain their integrity and are passed down through the generations until they degrade so far from the initial mystic core which sparked their development that they are completely devoid of mystic aliveness. At this point in the cycle of religious development there is a necessary death and rebirth so to speak.

From here, new prophets are born that help regenerate the authenticity of the religious traditions, which some members accept to while most others definitely do not. This splintering in the lineage tradition of each religion either creates sub-categories of the pre-existent religions or causes an entirely new religion to be formed. Through the many variations of configuration which result from these cycles, each religion organically formulates into a fundamentally valid expression of the mysteries of the cosmos presenting themselves to humanity over and over again. Equally so, every major movement of philosophical realization is a valid facet of the complexity of truth and every cultural movement is a valid reflection of the infinite variations of dynamic self-expression possible. (For the sake of discussion all of these aspects of society are being presented under the umbrella of religion)

In that light, all religions are the same truth which is eternally speaking through unique variations of cultural contexts. Humanity has undergone this cycle of religious tradition throughout the world time and time again.

In regards to the current major world religions, each of the primarily adopted traditions have all undergone multiple iterations of cycles with fractured variations worth noting.

True prophets such as Abraham, Ram, Krishna, Jesus, Mohammed, Lao Tzu, and Buddha, all caused a natural reinvigoration of the authentic connection to the spiritual core. They can be viewed as "beings who founded religions" or they can simply be viewed as beings that gave new life to spirituality in their given geographical regions and corresponding societies. The religious institutions created in their wake are led by worldly-minded beings who have naturally corrupted the traditions and divided the categories of belief again and again.

The spiritual core is carried forth regardless of the human degradation of these heritages.There have always been and will always be individuals whose spiritual experiences reintroduce the essence of truth into the traditions of teachings.

The original prophets of Judaism emerged spontaneously. Similarly, the original seers that lead to what is now known as Hinduism spontaneously arose, just like the mystic leaders of the Native beings to the land that is now known as America. The lineage of Judaism led to the development of Christianity and Islam, so in this sense, they can all be viewed as extensions of the same tradition. They can be viewed as branches of the same tree, perhaps even variations of the very same religion.

The original mystic beings of Hinduism were known as rishis or visionary seers. They also lead to this natural progression which fractured into Buddhism, Daoism, Jainism, the Sikh tradition, and so many more. They also can be viewed as branches of the same tree, or even variations of the exact same religion.

Even within a single tradition such as Buddhism, these cycles have come full circle through the traditions complete reinvention according to the people of different religions and eras. The appearance of Buddhism and the approach of the tradition has gone through a completed cycle of progression from Theravadan Buddhism to Mahayana Buddhism, Vajrayana and Zen to Pure Land.

This view of religious history is not meant to undermine the validity of any one of the factions of religion because there will always be value in the different religious approaches according to the different dispositions of mind. The development of the Religious Singularity is not about abolishing historical lineages, ending religions, nor making new religions necessarily. The Religious Singularity is merely an acknowledgement of the need for perfected harmony and a sense of one-ness amongst our planet's religions, cultures, and people.

The origins of the Sikh tradition is a phenomenal example of this progressive approach to religious development. Their tradition managed to merge two dominant religious systems which were previously at odds in their region. The Hindu and Muslim adherents spent many years warring and arguing until a series of authentic mystic seers starting with Guru Nanak came along and brought the two traditions into harmony by developing a singularity of religions which includes elements of both religious approaches. This is truly a feat worth applauding and an approach worth emulating as humanity moves forward.

Each of the world's religions is more and less effective at highlighting different aspects of the mystic truth which transcends language itself. As we continue along with the human project and seek to move past the ideologically driven conflicts which have spread throughout the planet, humanity will naturally develop new combinations of pre-existent religions and perhaps even invent entirely new systems of approach which draw on the same themes addressed by previous religions in a completely new way.

In reality, no religion needs to be undone and no new religion needs to be created nor fused together, but we must each find the approach that most fully speaks to us individually on our search for greater truth. To reach a point of religious harmony worldwide, we must stop linearly comparing one religion to another as no belief system will ever fully encapsulate all the aspects of reality entirely and some approaches work better for certain individuals more so than others. The same person may resonate more and less with different religions in their one lifetime. There should be no inhabitation or ideation of hierarchy in such a devotional and personal journey because language and belief will always be but a shadow of the truth.

The Buddha very aptly described this understanding with his teaching on the four philosophical extremes. He stated that there are four extremes of beliefs, all of which fall short at fully describing reality; however, when the four extremes are viewed collectively they may point at the spectrum of principles embodied by the universal essence which is beyond words, just as the collection of all religions may delineate the nature of phenomena more precisely than any one religion or philosophical movement can alone.

These philosophical extremes are: the affirmation that reality is existent, the negation of reality as non-existent illusion, the simultaneous belief in both God and Void, and the belief in neither existence (God) nor non-existence (Void). Many people falsely believe the Buddha to be been atheistic. However, in light of the teachings of the four philosophical extremes, it can be deciphered that the Buddha believed in transcending the traps of language and belief which distort our understanding of that which is beyond descriptors.

It's not that Buddha didn't believe in God, Buddha simply didn't believe in the implications that most assume when they hear the word "God".

The fundamental nature of phenomena is beyond describable qualities. Whether you choose to label it as God, Allah, Jah, Brahman, Void, Atman, Buddha-nature, Holy Spirit, Self, That-ness, Non-Self, or anything else, it is always the same essence of phenomena being discussed. From a surface level of investigation, it may seem like the teachings of each religion are separate or opposed, but in reality they are all complementary and can even deepen each other's meaning when viewed properly.

With this approach in mind, each of the world's religious teachings takes on new depth and meaning.

The goal of the Religious Singularity is not to eliminate all the religions of Earth or to formulate some new "master religion" which incorporates all previous religions, but to cultivate the view within all religious paths that each tradition is equally valid.

Religions are like different facets of the same diamond or different colors of the same rainbow. When the teachings of every religion can be recognized as complementary truths, then the goal of each religion will have been reached and the Religious Singularity will be achieved.

This singularity will bring an end to the countless debates of superiority and countless religious wars aimed at claiming spiritual dominance.

Of course, it will create space for new approaches to be forged, but this is not done in an attempt to further divide those of the various paths. Rather, these new hybrid religions will serve as bridges between the pre-established systems which will allow for greater clarity of the spectrum of approaches to understand the inner essence which unites us all.

Those who see only the material realm are like blind men feeling the different parts of an elephant. One religion is feeling the tusk saying God is smooth with a singular point at the end. Another religion is feeling the leg and saying God is made of many separate, scale-ridden bumps. Meanwhile, another religion is feeling the tail and saying that God keeps moving and therefore doesn't exist at all.

The truth can be best understood when we combine all the prophetic teachings of human history and begin to piece the puzzle together.

Each religion functions like the many rays emanating from the singular sun. The light shines through so many rays, but the source is always singular.

Don't worry about differences in the teachings until the essence underlying all of them becomes undeniably clear to you. Simply work with what makes sense to you personally and slowly the teachings will come together in your mind as a singular tapestry woven out of the seeming multiplicity.

The only real difference between the teachings in each of the world's religions are the words used to encompass the divine nature.

To collectively reach the point of Religious Singularity we must work backward from the ideal. Imagine what the world would look like if all religions were working together to enrich humanity's collective state.

We will never argue or debate ourselves into the singularity. We can only love one another into a point of mutual acceptance. Then, slowly, we will come to see how all the teachings and practices of the multitude of religious traditions work together to illuminate the essence of truth.

The point of Religious Singularity is about focusing on harmony for all humankind. This is the reason we have undergone the arduous journey of self inquiry in the first place. To reach such a point, tremendous compassion and patience will be required, but the possibility that peace could prevail on Earth makes it all worth our concern and contemplation.

7: THE ARCHETYPES

To fully understand the three pillars and their singularities, we have to imagine how each sphere would actually look in fully realized ideal of form. To understand our true potential in achieving agency as beneficial beings in the evolutionary track of Earth's globalized era we must look towards the great living and historical representations of leaders who most fully represent the ideals of our goals.

When investigating the first pillar, the Political Singularity, it can seem very difficult to establish clarity in regards to which system of governance and set of policies we should be working towards as there have been so few sustainable and completely compassionate historical examples to draw from.

Since we are exploring societal ideals of politics, it is natural to begin our inquisition with the work of Plato and his discourse on the philosopher king. Plato expressed that the ideal leader should be someone who is seeking truth and justice before personal gain, which he labeled as being a philosopher. This hierarchy of personal motivation being necessary for proper political leadership implies that the ideal leader will never be someone who is grasping for positions of power in the first place.

That implication of intent is the paradoxical qualification which makes this archetypal ideal quite difficult to authentically embody, let alone systematize to the point that it is beyond the reaches of an inevitable decay from corruption. This addendum to proper leadership is Plato's conceptual fail-safe for preventing the proposed leader from being overtaken by egoic intentions. When the use of tremendous personal will is necessarily required to obtain political power in the first place, how do you ensure that our leaders are being motivated by compassion in their orchestration of public policy? Despite the unlikely nature of a true philosopher king ascending to power in our institutionally corrupt modern political systems, it is the only way we will ever be able to properly transition to a truly harmonious era of international relations. This degree of self scrutiny will not only be required in the highest positions of power, but throughout the entire grid of human governance.

We may never have a true example of a philosopher king to look upon and model ourselves after, but it is something that all our political participants must strive for if we ever hope to establish peace on Earth. Studying this archetypal ideal of the philosopher king, the individual who embodies the essence of the Political Singularity, and striving to actualize compassion in politics in your own way in your own life is the only way for us to collectively avoid any future unwanted revolutions which would effectively restart the cycle of human suffering resulting from political quarreling.

The journey to reaching global stability while maintaining the necessary pillars of society is a winding and cyclical process. It should be obvious that each of the pillars has its own unavoidable role in our societal construction, but each individual inevitably holds a unique vision of which archetypal role within these systems of pillars that they personally will seek to embody in the course of their life's path.

Even within the individual archetypes, every person has a unique vision of what the ideal embodiment of that specific archetype even looks like in an embodied form. The pillar of technology is no exception. Every individual has a unique belief of what expressions of technology are essential to human life, which version of those inventions will be worth carrying forward into the unknown horizon of human history, and what potential configurations of integrating technology into our society may lay ahead in the greater arc of our collective evolution. This is perhaps true for the pillar of technology more so than any other because it is literally the pillar that represents innovation and invention, the next epiphany which is always beyond the reach of our current mind's knowing.

However we conceive of the innovations and regulations of production which will be required as our global society reach a point of functioning more ethically, it is unavoidably going to have to incorporate a few essential qualities. We have to the use our given natural resources in such a way that is sustainable and provides for the basic needs of the entirety of the human population.

The primary point of technology is to benefit its users, to create an ease of lifestyle, but if that ease of lifestyle for some is risking the well being of so many more than technology is by definition being used improperly. The merging of greater compassion into our innovative impulses is required for the Technological Singularity to occur. This compassion must acknowledge the delicate condition of Earth's environment while acknowledging the insatiable human inclination towards heightening our material well being. Weaving this complex array of aims together within the development of humanity's collective use of technology is not a task for the faint of heart. This infusion of compassion within innovation is true alchemy.

Maintaining conduciveness for human and environmental conditions while guiding invention to an ever-escalating state is the ultimate alchemy and the necessary equation to achieve the Technological Singularity properly. It is for this reason that the archetype of the Technological Singularity is known as the alchemist.

When we investigate the historical inventors and captains of industry, few examples were truly motivated by more than just financial gain. So many who have guided our journey with technology in the age of global materialism think little of environmental needs and even less of how their contributions alter the human condition. The archetype of the alchemist is always expressed uniquely relative to the time and place in which that individual lives and learns, as do all the archetypes of the respective pillars.

The most subtle sphere within the triad of singularities is the Religious Singularity. This singularity is difficult to define, and perhaps even to detect if it occurs fully because it doesn't necessarily require the invention of any new religions or the dismantling of any previous religious structures. This singularity merely requires the re-mystification of the current approaches and mutual acceptance between the factions of religions.

This particular singularity opens up a unique myriad of potential hazards in its development. The ego has easily manipulated the progression of religious evolution time and time again. Since this singularity doesn't inherently require any external signifiers to occur it creates a vacuum for those who materially replicate the symbols of spirituality to bypass the real self-effort required to achieve spiritual actualization and play dress up as a guru quite easily.

This is the dangerous disease that has kept the reality of the Religious Singularity from being achieved in previous moments of mass awakening such as the 1960s. It is very formulaic and simple to represent spirituality using external cues that imply the embodiment of spiritual ideals.

To achieve the Religious Singularity, there is no particular appearance of spirituality that will be required. Their is no uniform that proves you are the second coming of Christ or Maitreya Buddha. In fact, the true masters who embody the ultimate universal truths are so transcendent of external signifiers that they are completely undetectable to the untrained eye.

The true spiritual master may not follow any of the conventions that our human minds associate with any previous religion's qualifications of attainment. Within the traditional conventions of the world's major religions, there are clear signs of spiritual attainment according to the pre-determined rules which function within the individual religious lineages. However, living in the era of Religious Singularity will naturally create more ambiguity for the presentations of spiritual attainment as there is no fixed, external quality that can be viewed as a clear indication of spiritual realization. This leaves so much space for the egoic representation of enlightenment to dominant the religious landscape.

We have been living in the age of many fake gurus.

Not all of the current leaders of religion and spirit are falsely contrived, but a more highly discerning eye than ever before is required to navigate in these tenuous times. The convergence of monetary motivation and self-help programs is a fertile breeding ground for false prophets and charlatans to manipulate the majority of those seeking spiritual fulfillment.

To accommodate the intersectionality of the spiritual traditions comprising the Religious Singularity, this archetypal embodiment must be completely transcendent of categorical approaches which have dominated religion throughout human history. As each religion has different ideals of external qualifications, the archetype of the Religious Singularity will appear different relative to each tradition. There are, however, several internal signifiers that indicate the presence this archetype.

The true archetype of the Religious Singularity, the spiritual master, is someone who accommodates all religions and uplifts all well intending beings while avoiding excessively egoic motivation. The spiritual master always has a direct connection to the divine through their inner realms of vision and therefore maintain a sublime state of being.

The spiritual master is rarest of all archetypes in the modern world as they by definition are functioning in such as way that is beyond the traps of the delusive powers of the material world. It is easier to identify those who do not fulfill the totality of this archetype than it is to recognize a true spiritual master.

The spiritual master of the Religious Singularity is most likely embracing a formless path which consists of a direct and simple approach that brings people of all walks of life together in harmony and quietude. People of every religious tradition, every age, every race, and gender will flock to any true spiritual master to receive their silent blessings by experiencing their presence. This harmony of interaction in a spiritually explicit context is the most external of indications of the Religious Singularity in action.

The universal path of spiritual self-effort and inner attunement through meditation and prayer is a living bridge between all religions and paths. The archetype of the spiritual master is a complete hybrid of all the religious approaches because the essence lives through and transcends the bounds of them all.

Through the examples of the spiritual masters of the age of the Religious Singularity, each individual will naturally develop their own wakeful lifestyle that is completely and authentically unique to themselves.

As time progresses there will most likely be many iterations of the archetype of Religious Singularity at the different stages in the process of collective human development. Regardless of how it progresses, it is clear that we must all reach a mutual point of ideological acceptance to reach the era of global peace.

Within these three archetypes (the philosopher king, the alchemist, and the spiritual master), each individual will naturally find themselves embodying different levels and configurations of the pillars of ideals. We all have our inclinations of focus and should come to actualize our potential of lifestyle accordingly. There is no greater or lesser archetype or pillar within the journey to peace on Earth, every sector of society requires complete transformation for the Triadic Singularity to be achieved.

These are not the only archetypes in the vast construction comprising the entirety of creation; however, these are the archetypes whose fulfillment and embodiment will absolutely be required to usher in the golden era for humanity.

PART TWO:

THEIR SINGULARITY

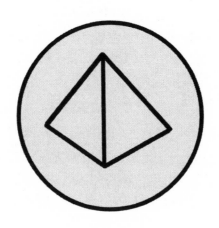

8: THREE AS ONE

Each pillar will undergo its own individual singularity, yet in turn the three will inherently harmonize into their own version of a singularity, the Triadic Singularity. The ever elusive enlightenment of society will only occur once all the spheres of singularities merge into a unified and functioning harmony. The true Triadic Singularity will arise as these three pillars of society converge through collective systems that work globally in tandem. This will require a significant number of individuals across the globe to step into the highest embodiments possible of their own unique variation of the eternal archetypes. As we attempt to help civilization achieve the heights of harmony, we each must personally strive to fulfill the lofty ideals within our own daily lives and actions.

Although the aspirations of the Triadic Singularity are global by design, their application and embodiment is always achieved through individual systems and personal approaches, then it spreads to the connected communities, and finally to the world as a whole. According to our unique dispositions, we each embody the different archetypes in varying degrees. However, in our individual efforts to achieve collective harmony, we will eventually have to grow into our own highest potential in every archetypal regard.

We must each strive to become our own version of a philosopher king, an alchemist, and a spiritual master. This can only be achieved relative to each of our roles within society but the principle holds as true nonetheless. Your every action creates the design in which your life plays out. The simplest shift in approach can make heaven of a hellish circumstance or vice versa. No matter who you are, what role you maintain in society, or how much power you wield, you will always have an opportunity to aspire towards the even higher potential which lies dormant in your here and now, always. No matter where you stand in the myriad of situations life provides, you have the potential, and therefore the responsibility, of striving towards your own highest archetypal embodiment.

You are already embodying each of these archetypes to greater and lesser degrees in each moment, whether you know it or not. You are the ruler of your own universe, the inventor of your own fate, and the mystic fulfilling your own spiritual destiny, all in this very instant.

You are the philosopher king, the alchemist, and the spiritual master as one already.

You are the three as one, the trinity of your own reality.

Nearly every religious tradition has reflected the three as one principle somewhere in their philosophy. The Christian tradition obviously addresses the Holy Trinity regularly. God as the Father, God as the Son, and God as the Holy Spirit are known to be one working through many facets. The Buddhists similarly teach of the three bodies of the Buddha nature. They are the aspects of the intelligence underlying all things, much like a notion of an omniscient God, and are called the Trikaya of the Dharmakaya, Sambhogakaya, and Nirmanakaya.

The Hindu tradition is known for worshipping God (Paramatman or Brahman) as having three primary aspects. These three embodiments are the same One God, although worshipped through three parts known as the Trimurti. The "three-as-one" of Hinduism are Brahma (the Creator), Vishnu (the Sustainer), and Shiva (the Regenerator).

The Trimurti, the aspects of energy that represent creating, maintaining, and transmuting or regenerating, sound a lot like the European philosopher, Immanuel Kant's, teachings of the dialectic. Kant teaches that every occurrence can be reduced to the process of a thesis meeting an antithesis and merging into a new synthesis. This Kantian dialectical view of reality is profoundly similar to the yogic teachings of creation, sustenance, and rebirth as represented abstractly by the Trimurti.

Despite these highly conceptual teachings about the various triads underlying the nature of existence, each religious tradition maintains teachings about individual beings who embody this archetypal singularity of triads as their one self.

The Christian tradition often speaks of Christ being the embodiment of the Trinity. The Hindu tradition teaches of Dattatreya, who is the incarnation of the Trimurti. Similarly, the Buddhist tradition teaches of Buddhas like Maitreya and Amitabha who embody the Trikaya (as well as the three jewels of the Buddha, Dharma, and Sangha).

It seems that nearly every culture idealizes different expressions of the same three as one philosophy of archetypal unity according to their model of language.

The goal of the Triadic Singularity is not to copy any of the descriptions you may read about these forthcoming prophets who exemplify the three primary archetypes within their individual self. See how you can actualize these ideals relative to your own role and your own historical placement with all of its preciously unique predicaments begging to be untangled. The fulfillment of your own role in the greater arc of our collective Triadic Singularity will inevitably be contextual, but this mass scale vision of global ideals can truly only happen by the hands of each individual.

No one has a monopoly on actualizing the essence of these archetypes or how they should look in ideal form.

We each must become our own version of Maitreya, of the return of Christ, or the re-incarnation of Guru Dattatreya, in each moment relative to our own lives and the needs of our own time.

How you grow into this potential is completely up to you, but the ultimate harmony between all the spheres of society on Earth will only develop as we do. How will you choose to serve, uplift, and embody the archetypal ideals echoing an enlightened society according to your own path? Whatever that may be, it is your key to our collective kingdom.

9: DEMONS, GODS, AND BODHISATTVAS

The journey to the actualization of your highest archetypal potentiality is the only effort that you can truly be sure will be of benefit in your attempts to help the world find balance. The complexity of the globalized era is more intricate than the human mind can decipher in a singular snapshot or even in a lifetime of contemplation. There will never be a human level thought or theory that is comprehensive enough to account for all the world's issues simultaneously. It is only through sustained focus and concerted effort towards uplifting the world in manageable ways that any lasting progress will occur.

There can certainly be councils and committees constructed to establish communal strides towards progress, but each action in life is made by the individual, even when performed in tandem with a community. In the process of attempting to better the state of global affairs, differing approaches will inevitably collide causing moments of unintentional conflict. One person's solution can at times cause another person's problems. Likewise, one person's ideal is another person's perception of imprisonment.

Although ethical ideals may be universal, the literal application of morality requires circumstantial subjectivity. As life continues to evolve, the complexity of things heightens the appearance of moral relativity. We all know in our emotional cores whether an action feels right or wrong to us, but life situations are seldom as binary as being merely right or wrong. Identifying actions as unquestionably right or wrong has, by in large, only further polarized humanity from finding a truly harmonious state.

Every single person, regardless of their moral actualization, is the hero in their own story. We all experience the story of life as being shown through our own eyes and told through the narrative of our own minds, so naturally we root for ourselves.

We are biological creatures, built through ages of evolution seeking survival and attempting to avoid threats. To fulfill this deep-seated urge for personal preservation, we all are encoded with an array of subtle psychological mechanisms that maintain our motivations, habits, and moral codes. Each has been justified through our conditioning which develops from our learned fears and desires.

There are a few beings that have actualized themselves to such a degree that they value the well beings of others as much as, if not more so than, their own comfort. For better or worse, this altruistic actualization in no way determines the effectiveness of one's influence over the collective state of humanity. Motivation is, in fact, often ego derived and as a result, the people who have the largest impact in the world are usually not those of the purest heart. Your agency in influencing society comes down to how much courage you have to create waves through the course of your life, not your degree of moral uprightness.

Nevertheless, even though courage may be the primary requisite to impress yourself upon the collective storyline, it is compassion that morally justifies your influence. So many people hide behind personal motivation, claiming their ends justify their means while they simultaneously create greater struggle for countless individuals in the wake of their misguided efforts. This is a common guise of fake righteousness which is alive and well in our degraded age.

The globalized era is highly interwoven with subtle and complex consequences to each of our actions that are often not immediately observable. We are all guilty of unintentionally, and sometimes intentionally, inflicting suffering upon others in the seeable and unseeable wakes of our activity. The balance of prioritizing the effect of our actions is often difficult to properly decipher.

Nonetheless, we must learn to focus our actions so that their consequences solely result in outcomes rooted in compassion for the entirety humanity's needs. We have to methodically engineer our activity to embrace the needs of all beings.

When we boil it all down to this level, it becomes quite obvious who the gods and who the demons are in this collective tale we are writing with the bloody ink of our days and lives.

Those who are tirelessly seeking to serve are on a divine path and those who let self-interest dominate their activity are the tormenters of humanity.

Plain and simple.

Your willingness to limit personal desire in acknowledgment of the needs of others determines the degree to which you are antagonistic or demonic in the grand play of the cosmos.

If your actions are causing others suffering, it is time to reevaluate your lifestyle.

Most people may not ever be willing to view themselves as a villain. Everyone likes to believe that they are justified in working towards their personal success and that no moral implications necessarily exist, but the wake of our actions speak for themselves. When you look at the total outcome of all the consequences of each of your actions, it is quite easy to see how much the well being of the collective has been kept in mind. With compassion as your north star, it is easy to tell the difference between those who wish to uplift humanity and those who are subjugating the masses as a result of their focus on personal desire.

The former are god-like, living Buddhas and Bodhisattvas.

The latter are selfish, and therefore literally demonic.

Moral relativity creates an easy hiding place for the self-interested. We can all identify as well-meaning people, but if compassion isn't the primary force determining your path then you are engaging in self-deception far more than you are willing to recognize.

Finding the path of compassion is a never-ending journey, it requires self-evaluation with every step. It is not a problem to make mistakes as long as you learn the true impact of your actions and swift self-reformation is engaged.

We must lift humanity up, even at the cost of our own comfort.

Universal maxims of right and wrong actually do exist when it comes to eliminating suffering. We as a species must learn to function with a basic level of goodness. In a detached manner, we must slowly dismantle the institutionalized systems of approach which reinforce suffering until every single sentient being can experience peace as a norm throughout their lifetimes.

Let us aspire to fulfill our divine potential and become the gods we were born to be.

The pressures of the modern world have led so many into the strata of inflicting suffering on one another. Seeking monetary well being is a requirement for modern living we all must face. Our competition-based system reinforces the survivalist mentality been propelled our collective journey as a species thus far. Generational wealth is a similarly self-perpetuating organism. It's incestuous. Hoarding resources and creating scarcity for others doesn't solve our collective problems in any sense, in fact it only adds to the tensions of economic disparity and corresponding violence. Greed actually ends up worsening the quality of life for everyone over time.

There are a few powerful individuals who have achieved success through different avenues of society that have come to recognize the need for reciprocity in our attempts to ensure a state of mutual well being. From non-profits focused on serving the disenfranchised, to policymakers creating actually beneficial laws and programs, to cultural revolutions oriented to benefit the whole of humanity: there have been many kind-hearted efforts in human history which are slowly starting to counteract the institutionalized greed that has been dominant for so long.

Loving-kindness and compassion are unavoidably necessary to develop world peace. Programs and policies promoting and even enforcing altruism are inevitable progressions that will continue to grow in correlation with the evolution of our species and the natural integration of human compassion into human governance.

We must each do whatever is in our capacity to support those who suffer if we wish to collectively survive the impending calamities facing humanity. Everyone is left more enriched by not leaving the downtrodden of society in perpetual turmoil. If we wish to live free of protest, looting, uprising, and revolution then we must systematically uplift the less fortunate.

Serving humanity is serving yourself. This is the essence of the Bodhisattva principle. Through altruism the few pure-hearted individuals who have had success within our competition-based system, those who see the downfalls of greed and ego driven activity, harmony will eventually be achieved on a global scale.

It's a slow process. It will require those with political influence to use their power to help those without a voice, those with cultural notoriety to use their platform for promoting the needs of the unnoticed, and those with technology that betters the quality of life to help provide that same experience for those who lack it. You don't have to be rich or formally volunteer for a charity to give a meal to someone who is homeless or hungry. One of the most radically transformative acts in our self-interested world is to simply feed people.

The controlling powers may try to promote disunity amongst the people, but compassion is unavoidable when a human witnesses another human who is suffering.

There will always be uprisings of compassion as long as needless suffering occurs, no matter what empire is in power.

There will also always be Bodhisattva-like beings because many humans will always feel the inner urge towards kindness, even in the direst of circumstances.

No matter how we twist the story with our minds and our defense mechanisms, our character and the archetype we embody is solely determined by the culture of our activity. How do you choose to spend your days and in what ways does your touch sculpt the world at large?

You are creating a legacy with your every move, your every breath. Can you comfortably proclaim that you are beckoning the triad of singularities in this lifetime?

10: THE MASTER KEY

Throughout the expanse of human history, every single war has been mentally justified by those participating.

In reality, subjugating others will never actually relinquish our suffering.

Suffering first transpires within, it is not solely a product of outer circumstance. To treat each other with the necessary level of dignity required to properly stabilize a global society, we must learn to cultivate the unshakable heights of our dormant inner compassion.

We must learn to systematically uproot our aggression and craft a new schema of fully realized, universal compassion above all else.

With the endless onslaught of hostile influences bombarding us throughout our lives, it may seem impossible to learn to live fully in a fully compassionate state of consciousness.

There is no easy way around the rewiring, reparenting, and reconditioning of our response patterns until we can each perpetually function in total compassion.

We must tenaciously study the techniques and practice the disciplines that allow for a newfound inner mastery. This will require profound dedication to the discipline of retraining the mind.

Essentially, the master key to all of the world's problems is a pretty obvious notion.

To establish peace on earth we must each learn to cultivate unmoving peace within ourselves.

The key to balancing all of our complicated outer systems is that we each must cultivate supreme inner clarity. To foster peace in the outer world, we must first learn to foster peace within ourselves.

A tremendous amount of discipline will be required to establish total inner peace.

A vigilant eye must be maintained.

To create peacefulness within our political systems, between those engaged in religious feuds, and those participating in the misuse of technological power we must each evolve into more fully self-mastered versions of our selves.

Evolution is forged through the intelligent impulse living within us all which navigates us through the challenges at hand in any given circumstance.

This is the fundamental notion of the evolutionary impulse taken to its most essential form.

The evolutionary path, which has taken our species through so many gauntlets of opposition externally, must now turn in upon itself.

The greatest threat to the survival of our species is now our own greed and egoistical divisiveness.

To properly evolve through the impending scarcity of resources, threats from nuclear technology, and generally looming environmental calamity, we must learn to work together fully. This will absolutely require mastery over our lower impulses. The only way to ensure our outer destiny is to learn to harness our inherent intelligence within.

To understand the evolutionary path forward, we must understand the nature of the evolutionary impulse itself.

Evolution is a product of the indwelling intelligence which exists fundamentally throughout nature. Even basic cellular organisms intelligently evolve because intelligence is fundamental.

Intelligence is an appendage of pre-existent, indwelling consciousness. Consciousness is more fundamental to our universe's construction than most have yet to realize.

It is, in fact, more fundamental than matter.

Consciousness is the essence of reality.

Consciousness created all that can see and all that can be seen, by the force of its own intelligent nature.

The implication of studying the natural path of evolution is that reality maintains a degree of inherent consciousness regardless of composition of the degree of complexity embodied by its organisms.

Consciousness exists inherently in all things which implies that there is a unified field of collective consciousness which underlies reality as we know it. Consciousness in part is like a web which reality's functions are immersed within, as an autonomous and omnipresent intelligence which is often referred to with labels such as God, Allah, Paramatman, or Buddha nature.

It actually doesn't matter which name that you choose to attribute to the indwelling intelligence because it is beyond all limitations of mind and language.

What does matter is the acknowledgment of the indwelling intelligence that has guided, and will continue to guide, the invisible path of our collective evolution.

This recognition infers that to continue evolving in correspondence with this indwelling consciousness, we must learn to intentionally evolve our personal intelligence through the refinement of our conscious awareness as a reflection of the essence of the collective arc of evolution which has brought us to this point as a species.

The process of intentionally refining intelligence is considered the training of the mind. To successfully continue on the path of evolving as species, which has reached this most critical stage where our species functions with self-reflective recognition, we must now take the reins of our intelligence actively by practicing the art of controlling our own minds.

The only way to fully ensure the mastery of mind and consciously controlling our own inner awareness is through meditation.

Meditation is the only path to ensure our ability to regulate our intelligence and to intentionally generate the compassion necessary to continue on our evolutionary journey as a species.

Meditation is the master key to evolution.

Meditation is the core of what has led to all of the spiritual teachers achieving mastery throughout history.

They each recognized the same indwelling intelligence, the same essential truths, and embodied their own personal peaks of actualizing the one cosmic intelligence.

Mind control through meditation leads us to the essence reality, beyond form, which has the subtle qualities of pure being, pure intelligence, and fundamental joy which have all secretly guided our evolution along the way.

Attuning to this consciousness beyond the mind using the mind itself through meditation leads to profound insight beyond what discourse or introspection ever could.

We are all tapped into the same intelligence, which has guided the entirety of evolution, but only through meditation can we fully invoke the evolutionary force of the intellect to its ultimate potential.

There are many approaches and styles of spiritual discipline which can help to increase this connection to the indwelling intelligence, but at all of their roots is meditation.

Meditation is the unbroken connection to the substratum of intelligence and to the core of evolution itself.

Thus far we have stumbled through the course of evolution, but when you engage in mind control through meditation you become one with the source of all evolution.

Through meditation, you merge with the divine.

As the Bible clearly states, the kingdom of heaven is within you. The only way to transcend our suffering is to learn the techniques of mind control.

Meditation is the great mediator of all aspects of life. It regulates mind, body, and emotion through skillful means because it activates the indwelling intelligence of evolution, it invokes the consciousness laying dormant on the deepest of levels.

End your suffering by learning to turn within and attune to the blissful intelligence which is your birthright. This will be your master key to the eternally enlightened kingdom dwelling within you. In due time, you will bring this inner castle of light into the world in so many delightfully unimaginable ways.

As you begin the path of meditation, do not cling to any expectations of achieving enlightenment.

Simply meditate for the inherent value of meditation. You cannot actually attain enlightenment, you can only unattained un-enlightenment.

Enlightenment is the natural state of consciousness.

We are all born enlightened. We all come from vast realms of light and divine consciousness. Slowly over the course of our lives, we slip into identification models that prevent us from accessing the natural state of enlightenment.

The ego is a necessary aspect of a functioning mind that has, thus far, prevented you from knowing that enlightened intelligence has been hiding within you all along.

To shed the confines of our limited perspectives, we must dive each day into the limitlessness of inner awareness.

Slowly our awareness will be purified through daily meditation and we will return to fully identifying as pure consciousness.

Slowly through daily meditation, we can return to our naturally enlightened state.

The cosmic humor of it all is that even though infinite intelligence is our natural state, the ego automatically veils this from our awareness.

Even though there is nothing more natural than enlightenment, it requires an intense and regular meditation practice to undo all our conditioning in such a way that enlightenment bleeds into our every motion effortlessly.

Enlightenment is our origin and our destiny.

The purity of the divine is always being reflected in us and through us, but the dirt and dust of human incarnation collect on the mirror of our minds with each passing day.

This is why we must regularly clean the mirror.

This is why we must make daily spiritual disciplines have a habitual role in our lives.

The more we know enlightenment to be natural, the more we must (seemingly paradoxically) take on the rigor of daily meditation practice.

This is an unspoken law of cosmic consciousness.

What is preventing humanity from achieving global harmony and synchronized interconnected politically?

Ego.

What is preventing humanity from functioning in perfect union with our technological capabilities and available resources?

Ego.

What is preventing humanity from fully accepting one another's beliefs without holding any feelings of malice or any sense of emotional dissonance between the participants of religious practices and cultural proclivities?

Ego.

The only way to completely master ourselves is to learn to keep our egos in submission relative to our true selves.

The only way to fully gain control of the ego, which is a wonderful servant and a terrible master, is to gain complete control over our own minds.

As we learn to master our minds we will learn to master ourselves and, in turn, learn to serve humanity's evolution to the utmost of our personal capability.

Recognizing that meditation is the master key of evolution, let us now investigate its most essential technique and a few tips to bring ease to the path.

To begin, become aware of your natural body-consciousness.

We all have a subconsciously rooted, spatial awareness of our bodies and the area just around them. This is how we can walk with our eyes closed or in the dark. This spatial awareness is a subconscious configuration of the mind which can be made conscious.

Our consciousnesses are automatically linked to that spatial awareness, so to maintain our natural orientation of awareness in meditation, it makes sense to work with the natural orientation of our bodies.

The implication here is the role of posture in practicing meditation.

We are bipedal organisms that have grown to walk, and primarily keep the spine upright and erect. This means the ideal posture for meditation requires us to sit upright, if possible.

Laying down can indeed help the mind relax, but it also more quickly drags the mind over the meditative line and into a state of sleep.

What is the difference between sleep and meditation? Well, one is a conscious rest and the other is an unconscious state of rest, so the line is very thin.

This all the more adds value to maintaining a wakeful posture which reinforces the alertness of meditating with a spatial awareness that is held akin to if you were walking normally, but in this case, you will be seated with your eyes closed.

Do not fret or attach too entirely to these ideals of posture if you are unable to sit perfectly still. It is best to maintain a non-attached attitude and to calmly adjust your posture as needed throughout your meditation practice.

Don't be too hard on yourself.

Ideally, you can adjust your body while maintaining your inner focus on the meditation without having to open your eyes or break the connection to your inner awareness while your subconscious spatial awareness simply shifts according to your need.

Once your posture is established, draw your awareness from the sense organs into the sphere of your mind. This is often done through your days when deeply contemplating or concentrating without most people even realizing it.

Since sight is a dominant mode of perception, just as you have fixed your posture in alignment with the natural mode of spatial awareness, the next step is to align your inner sight with the natural orientation of your eyes.

In meditation, fix your gaze as if you are looking straight ahead with your eyes closed. Simply find the point, with your eyes closed, where the sightlines of your eyes naturally meet.

This will be somewhere near, perhaps slightly above, the point between your eyebrows.

Keeping your eyes singularly focused on this point is the best method of mind control as it is the natural position from which you evolved to perceive with sight.

Your mind will naturally wander, but keep coming back to fix your gaze on this point between the eyebrows.

This simple technique is known to many as third eye meditation.

This point is merely the natural place of concentrative alignment based on the biological course of evolution.

The importance of third eye meditation specifically is that it is the technique which allows for the complete development of mind control. If you meditate on your heart or other primary energy centers of the body you will dissolve into bliss and have a healing experience, but eventually your mind will creep back in and bring you back to your body (effectively ending your immersion in the meditation experience). However, if you achieve the bliss and transcendence of meditation through the third eye than your mind will remain under your control and you can stay in meditation longer.

You don't have to believe in chakras to see how this point is the natural place where a wakeful yet resting awareness would align for bipedal beings that visually perceive through the eyes.

Make the point between your eyebrows the resting place of your mind, this is the best way to ensure mind control which will gradually lead to inner calm and peacefulness.

The development of that inner-attuning muscle of concentration will inevitably lead to a greater faculty for outer peace, kindness, and compassion.

A few tips to increase your attentiveness to this point between your eyebrows: gently press your tongue to the roof of your mouth, ever so slightly tilt your head back so your eyeballs aren't straining to lock into this position of focus, and slightly curl the sides of your lips in a gentle smile which orients the muscles in your face to concentrate upon this central position and indicates to your body that it is alright to relax.

If you catch yourself thinking, just bring your awareness back to the point between the eyebrows without any comment or judgment.

If you wish to dissociate from your thoughts and are having trouble doing so, you can mentally label your thoughts as they arise with the word 'thinking' or 'mind'.

This will help you return to the meditative state at the stages where you are still building the muscle of impulse which will allow you to return to meditation without any thoughts (which is ideal).

Similarly, you can use prayer or other affirmations to direct your mind to a meditative state.

By clearly affirming to the mind that you are going to enter a state of meditation, it helps the subconscious relax into the state.

The simple act of praying for good meditation is also shockingly effective when done from a sincere place of aspiration.

Every fifteen to twenty minutes, the mind's resting state naturally deepens and further dissolves into the meditation awareness.

The implication here is that after about an hour, and every subsequent hour you consecutively meditate after that, your awareness noticeably deepens.

Any style and posture of meditation possible are good to start, be it guided or not, but you will naturally notice how meditations incrementally deepen with continuous time and regular practice.

You cannot force this relaxed alertness.

You simply must attune into it and slowly grow the muscle of willfully entering the meditation state.

After years of practice, it will be as natural as eating or breathing, and you will be able to fully dissolve your mind into meditation upon command.

Perhaps you will even reach the point where it is accessible instantaneously.

If you meditate twenty to forty minutes each day your life will be filled with peace and the extremes of mind, body, and emotion will be brought into balance.

However, if you seek to know the most profound depths of inner truth, and receive unspeakably delightful inner visions, you should begin practicing meditation for an hour or more each day.

Most of the meditation masters of history have been known to sit between two and twelve hours daily depending on their circumstances, degree of insight, and stage of training.

No matter how much you engage in meditation, it will vastly increase your peacefulness and serve your ability to be a force of compassion in the world.

Meditation is the key to developing your compassion which you will automatically bring to the world at large when your heart has been truly purified.

Meditation is the greatest technology that will grant our species the ability to heal from our collective disharmony. Meditation will teach you to calm the turbulences within yourself, thus enabling you to calm the turbulences of society at large.

If we wish to survive as a species let alone achieve a level of harmonious functioning as a globally interconnected society in this extremely complicated age, we must create a normalized culture of meditation worldwide.

We've had the key in our back pocket all along.

Meditation will teach us to save ourselves from destructive mentalities and emotions and shows us the inner ailments which will in turn allow us to act in such a way that we help save each other from the destructive repercussions of our collectively animalistic instincts.

Meditation is the ultimate expression of evolution and it will bring our journey as a species full circle.

We dove headfirst into the biological world and now, to swim back to the surface of divinity, we must learn to master the intelligent impulse of evolution through meditative mind control.

After great focus on the myriad of complex problems preventing society from fully passed evolving our negatively implicating external patterns, the reality that the most important factor needed for global healing being internal has finally become clear.

There is no other way to ride the waves of the singularities to their undeniable crest of cultivating a true Heaven out of Earth.

11: LOWERING THE DRAWBRIDGE

No matter how much meditation you practice daily, every single moment of true attunement to your innermost essence has an infinitely beneficial effect on your well being. The inner spaciousness of meditation is the fertile ground which allows the seeds of your intentions to grow into an increased agency to make a difference in the world.

A few moments, a few minutes, a few hours: whatever amount of meditation you can manage to experience is worth your effort.

Every glimpse of peacefulness is carried with you throughout your days. A single instant of inner calm and meditative attunement will fundamentally redirect the nature of each of your actions that follow and your entire path in life that ensues as a result.

Inner peace is your greatest armor for the daily battles of worldly struggle which constantly pervade the realms of being human.

No matter which role you inhabit within society, your performative ability will be heightened by introducing regular meditation into your lifestyle. Every societal role is tremendously benefited through the increased inner clarity which unfolds naturally through meditation practice. In this way, through the evolutionary journey of each individual's spiritual development, society as a whole is organically transformed and benefited in countless ways both immanent and mysteriously elusive. Every sector of society is being enriched relative to its own needs as the practicing culture of meditation normalizes globally.

Meditation helps people from all walks of life.

Imagine how benefitted prisoners would be from receiving proper meditation training. Not only would meditation make the difficult circumstances of being imprisoned more bearable, but it would also serve in helping the previously incarcerated handle the confusing transition back into society. Much like how meditation development services would serve the transition for soldiers returning to civilian life after being in a war zones.

Police brutality is a major issue in many of the major cities and towns worldwide. If the police were trained in meditation, their levels of calm and self control would be greatly increased and the instances of police brutality would therefore naturally decrease. Of course, there should also be laws put in place to dissuade police from using guns as a first resort as well as further police training in de-escalation and more complete education regarding systemic racism to combat this continuing pattern with police. However, teaching the police how to regulate themselves through meditation is an absolutely necessary first step if we wish to eradicate the growing disease of police brutality.

Being a police officer is probably a very nerve-wracking job. Meditation would help calm their nerves and handle each situation with heightened mindfulness and care, even when they feel threatened, which would in turn give them greater clarity in how to properly handle those difficult situations.

Politicians would certainly be benefitted from meditation. There are so many complicated decisions that have to be made by lawmakers. The inner clarity received through meditation would certainly help them with their decision and policy making, which affects the lives of us all. Through the heightening of awareness which occurs organically through meditation, compassion also naturally heightens as we witness and truly contemplate the vastness interconnecting us and universality of human suffering. These are is an invaluable contemplations for a human being, but it is especially necessary for our lawmakers to cultivate extreme levels of compassion to properly guide their decision making. As we see more clearly and exist in a more calm and centered state, it becomes more difficult to avoid our inner consciences. Meditation leads to introspection in such a way that naturally evokes heightened morality. A politician committed to meditation is more likely to feel authentically moved by the suffering of their constituents to the point of working towards justice than a politician who doesn't meditate.

Many executives are turning to meditation to help with the stress of their fast-paced lives, but you don't have to work in a high-stakes corporate environment to practically benefit from meditation. Individuals on every level of the economic ladder are all benefitted by practicing meditation. So much of our society is run by people working mind-numbing jobs that they often despise. Perhaps someday many these jobs will be automated, but for now, many workers have to deal with the monotony of unending boredom from performing menial tasks. Meditation and the many techniques associated with meditation which increase mindfulness are great means to help regulate our mindsets and emotional status to the point that even the most boring of jobs can be made a platform to bask in a joyous and contented state.

Scientists and entertainers alike are constantly required to manufacture creative solutions to complex situations. Although these professions seem to be polar opposite by design, they equally depend upon flexing the mental muscles of innovation and inventiveness. Meditation reawakens your access to a mindset which is bursting with inspiration. Anyone who occupies these professions, and so many others, would all be undeniably benefitted from the practice of meditation.

Whether you are a teacher having to deal with the difficult task of conveying ideas while balancing the excitable energies of the youth, or a priest who must regularly draw upon deep and contemplative ideas, you will be benefitted greatly by taking on a daily meditation practice.

Meditation makes lovers more present and empathetic towards one another. It increases the ability to feel and be felt, to know and share love. Meditation makes parents more capable of relating to their children's needs while maintaining the inner clarity required to keep a sense of autonomy and sanity in the whirlwind of raising kids.

Meditation helps kids in their journey to finding themselves while navigating the unexpected curveballs that life throws all our ways. Young or old, rich or poor, whether you are a member of any religion or an atheist: meditation will uplift your life in endless ways, known and unknown.

We are the stones building the great pillars of an enlightened society. We are the chosen ones riding the wave of perfect timing into the age of singularities in every sector of society. We are the ones who will rise through the broken approaches of yesteryear. We are the ones who must master ourselves and bring our newfound sense of reality to all the damaged systems and sorrowful roles being played out in our collective human drama.

No matter which role or archetype you embody, there is always room to grow into a higher expression of that form. Through the practice of meditation, you slowly elevate the version of yourself that you have come to embody.

No one would not be benefitted from a lifestyle that includes daily meditation.

Each role can be elevated in its degree of actualization. Every being is the divine intelligence in a disguise hiding from ourselves. We are all waiting for the spark of inner light to be fanned and brought back ablaze with bliss.

Meditation is the gust of wind which ignites and expands your inner flame.

It will bring your inner vision and identity back to life. As your inner divinity is fully recognized by your conscious mind, your outer life will synchronize its form to unfold the most magical kingdom of your own very heaven in each moment. When you stand fully in your inner kingdom, the outer mandala of a more sacred world will naturally dawn with your every step and breath.

Meditation is the master key to the kingdom.

This is how you open the gate and begin to lower the drawbridge for the kingdom of Heaven to become accessible on Earth.

12: SUMMONING SHAMBALA

Haven't we had quite enough of making Earth into a hellscape for one another?

When will we reach the breaking point of being so selfish every which way until the world bleeds?

It is sickening to see the business as usual mentality bringing humanity to its knees.

We must each work tirelessly to rectify the horror of what humanity has done to our Earth and each other, to undo the violence which has dominated our species generation after generation since time immemorable.

It was only natural that our primate ancestors were afraid and fought for their claim in life. It's only natural that our tribal ancestors were afraid and fought, too. But now we have come so far, had so many revolutions and chances for peace, yet still the forces of greed and egotism have still found a manipulative stronghold to keep us all pacified. The deception is so ingrained in our lives and systems of society that even mass protests and worldwide movements for peace haven't been able to flip the script.

Yet we have come too far to give up now.

We have to do everything in our power to maintain wakefulness and peace throughout our days. We perhaps have to do even more than that, it seems, to bring wakefulness and peacefulness to our entire population.

Cultivating a world of peace is no easy task. We certainly can't fight for peace, but perhaps we can will it.

Our screams haven't been heard, but perhaps our diligent efforts will prevail nonetheless if we persist.

Now is no time for becoming disheartened as we are actually on the cusp of being more than just another failed animal species whose hubris hails mass extinction.

The task at hand is to achieve mastery over ourselves so entirely that the flow of harmonious occurrences in our lives spreads and spreads until all the people playing all the parts throughout the land have their inner thirst quenched too.

It is not enough to attain enlightenment, but we must all vow to serve each others' awakenings as well. We must become an entire society built upon wakeful compassion if we wish to make it through the trials ahead.

It is for this cause that the notion of the Triadic Singularity has been presented.

Each of the spheres of society are unavoidably coalescing on a mass scale and consequentially intertwined to the Nth degree.

We can't back down now.

It is easy for people to demonize the government, the major world religions, and the globally excessive production of technology and use of the non-renewable resources. It is a lot more difficult for us to authentically make the most of the systematic foundations in place and work with the current construct of institutions that has been meticulously been curated over the course of recent human history until they are transformed into more ideal forms rather than merely destroyed for their imperfect organization.

Let us build upon the pillars as they stand.

Let us build upon on ourselves as we stand, although the true effect of meditation and self-work can be more aptly related to a dismantling of the false self.

Somehow, someway, we must sculpt the government to serve the needs of the people. We uncover the brilliantly illuminated truths buried in our antiquated religious traditions until they come back to life. We must learn to properly harness the power of technology and not let it destroy us in the process.

The singularity within each of the three pillars must be achieved in individual sectors, but in the harmonious alignment of the major spheres of society a glorious unity of global peace will follow.

Although achieving a globalized expression of the Triadic Singularity would be an unspeakably profound feat, it wouldn't necessarily be the first example of an enlightened society existing in Earth's history. We have all heard tales of King Arthur, the knights of the round table, and Camelot. Most of us have also heard different iterations of the lost city of Atlantis.

If either of these civilizations existed, they have certainly come and gone. Nonetheless, we have sketches of our ideals which lay before us and can guide us, at least in our intent, to attaining greater heights as a of civilization.

Many who are reading this book may not have heard of Ayodhya or the Raghu dynasty, however, it is another profound example of the ideals being discussed. In the region which is now known as India, there was once a hyper-functional society where uprightness and spirituality operated fully. The rulers of this dynasty were known as the Raghus and the crowned jewel of this lineage was named Rama. Rama was born enlightened, became king, and is said to have had access to technology that seems relatable to modern planes and even nuclear weapons.

Lord Rama is known to be a paramount expression of all the spheres of society working in unison, so much so that the entirety of the population inhabiting his land were supposedly living in peace.

Taking this discourse into the realm of what many may call speculation, there has recently been evidence of radioactive material on the surface of Mars that could have been caused by a nuclear meltdown tens of thousands of years ago. Some believe this is the remains of an advanced civilization that had exquisite enough technology to bring the individuals to Earth, which led to the birth of our distant ancestors.

It is impossible to confirm that any of these examples are anything more than mythology or lore, but they are at least worth contemplating as abstract inspiration for the project of envisioning the formation of an enlightened society according to modern ideals.

What would a singularity of the world's political structures, major religions, and technological sector even look like?

Imagine a world where humanity is beyond war, beyond unnecessary suffering, and in harmony with the planet and all its creatures.

What a beautiful dream to dream.

In Tibet, their entire societal structure was built on this vision, which they have labeled Shambala. Some believe Shambala is yet to come and other prophecies indicate an enlightened society which already existed. Others believe Shambala is a non-physical realm, like a heavenly afterlife with the Buddha awaiting.

A similar place, called the Pure Land, is described in other Buddhist scriptures. Governed by a Buddha, even the trees in the Pure Land glisten like gems and whisper the secrets of enlightenment.

It is easy to write all these examples off as fairy tales. It is even easier to give up on the potential of our species making it through this most agitated of eras, but there doesn't seem to be a more noble intention than to bring a heavenly repose to our earthly human tragedies.

The real Shambala is hidden in plain sight.

Anywhere a Buddha inhabits is the realm of Shambala.

When you walk in wakefulness, you summon Shambala.

Ancient Egyptians and Mayans were said to have reached a degree of embodying the Triadic Singularity each respectively. They also both built physical pyramids as manifestations reflecting their hope of literally bringing heavenly realms to our earthly abode.

Unfortunately, the heights of these civilizations' reigns have come and passed.

Perhaps by building the non-physical pyramid constructed with the three pillars of singularities, our next true attempt at achieving peace on Earth will last a bit longer.

However hard we try, society's liberation will always start with individual self-mastery.

So, that task deserves greater exploration by each of us if we actually expect the world at large to follow suit.

PART THREE:

TAKING FLIGHT

13: REVERSING POLARITY

To better understand our true place in the cosmos and how to create a society that is aligned with it, we need to better understand the nature of the cosmos itself. The natural course of any life form's energy over time is decay. Our planet, solar system, and even universe will eventually decay much like the human body. In fact, the entirety of creation naturally expanded and will just as naturally collapse back into an immaterial state eventually.

With the recognition of consciousness as the intelligent essence of evolution, we can interpret the procession of the cosmos with even greater insight than the modern scientific inquiry has yet to provide. Dissecting the expansion of the universe, in relationship to the evolution of matter as it relates to consciousness, provides keen insight into the chain of events that have led to this point and which will also carry evolution forward through the rest of time.

Energy in its purest state is consciousness, beaming with intelligence. As energy densifies into matter, the indwelling intelligence slowly loses the strength of connection to that state of pure luminosity. As this energy is slowly distorted to take on the forms of elements, celestial bodies, objects, and entities, its intelligence also shifts identification from unity with the whole of existent energy to the specific form in which it is inhabiting. This shift to relative identification can be viewed as the source of the ego.

Space, and the vacuum of luminous emptiness therein, has condensed itself into particles. This phenomenon has caused the formation of elemental compounds that eventually developed into biological beings.

This compounding of energy concentration over eons has led to the separate life forms that we as humans inhabit. Through the cohesive power of love which is the glue that underlies creation, endless iterations of formations of self have transpired. This bonding and binding power of love has allowed the universe to explore its own vastness through many forms, but it also inherently led to separate identification and the suffering which arises thereafter.

We are a great example of how identification assumes the form it inhabits over the course of evolution. Each human thinks of themselves as the identity connected to the body through which they function. The same is true for energy on each level of incarnation, be it animal, planetary body, elemental, celestial entity, or otherwise. This is what is meant by the densification of energy being the source of ignorance. As long as we identify with any relative aspect of form more so than the whole of intelligent energy, we will remain subject to suffering.

The process of intentionally identifying with consciousness more than any form it inhabits causes the reversal of the evolutionary densification process. How do you reverse the polarities of energy's evolution and shift from the densification of matter to the expansive luminescence of human consciousness?

When you actively identify with consciousness and merge your awareness with consciousness through meditation, you reach the turning point of evolution.

Thus far our collective evolution has been governed by the slow decay of intelligence through the narrowing of identification into the relatively microscopic level of biological incarnation. When you actively use your will to unite awareness with pure consciousness, you take the reins of evolution into your own hands and enter into the next phase of the evolutionary journey. You enter into the realms of Angels and Buddha.

Many spiritual disciplines are ways of activating this reversal of polarity, but the root of each is meditation. Meditation is the act of consciously merging with the intelligent substratum of reality, the union with radiant formlessness.

Meditation itself is the pure state of enlightenment, of Buddha nature, of Christ Consciousness, of Parambrahman, of Allah. It is the key to your awakening and journey towards embodying your primordial nature as enlightenment made flesh.

However, the essence of this fundamentally empty yet luminous intelligence underlying phenomenon must be brought actively into each of the aspects and spheres of life as a whole if the project at hand is to actually bring forth a heavenly state within the regions of Earth. Spiritual practices, disciplines, rituals, techniques and subtle technologies are all applied forms of this meditative essence. Spiritual activity is the literal process of bringing evolutionary intelligence back into matter.

Active engagement in spiritual discipline reverses the polarities from energetic decay to energetic regeneration.

Perhaps you have seen different examples reflecting this principle like when monks and saints bodies naturally do not decay for days, weeks, months, or even years after their deaths.

The true effect of spiritual discipline is the movement away from identification with separateness and towards identification to the point of constant communion with the infinite.

With the awareness of the infinite comes the intelligence and wakefulness of the infinite.

Energy is always fundamentally enlightened, but by shifting our limited focus to the limitlessness of inner realms we merge our awarenesses with this enlightened intelligence.

In your movement towards assuming enlightenment, you are fulfilling the grandest arc of evolution. This process of using your will to awaken to your divine potential within in this very lifetime will make what you once knew as Earth become your very own Heaven.

This level of identification and perception will initially take tireless effort to be naturalized in your sense of being.

You cannot simply continue living as you have been living and truly expect Earth to suddenly become Heaven.

The transformation must be engaged in and embraced on every single level of your life. You have to be honest with yourself and adjust your life according to your intuition continually.

This reversal of polarities is all about taking your human activity into the strata of Buddha activity, Angelic activity.

To make Earth into a divine abode, you must take your human habits into the spheres of heavenly habits. The core of this process is meditation, but for it to be fully actualized this conclusion must permeate every arena of your post-meditation activity as well. This will require radical self-study and perpetual aspiration.

Just as attending university requires intensive study of any given curriculum if it is to be understood, your enlightenment will require similarly intensive efforts towards self-study.

Your spiritual practices are the direct force that determines your evolution from here on out. They are the vehicles in which you will take flight, but also they are each literal microcosms of direct qualities of the universe. The practices are like a map of God's mind and like a mysterious puzzle whose hidden image is the key to your enlightenment.

You can view the spiritual practices themselves as literal reflections of the cosmos.

Everything in existence functions within patterns, sliding scales of cycles, and therefore according to the principle of the fractal: the microcosmic realms are always reflecting patterns from the macrocosmic realms.

Traditional spiritual practices were not chosen arbitrarily.

You will come to know the cosmological procession of energy densification as a mirror of the mind through practicing spiritual disciplines. Each of the stages of densification are directly relatable to the different paths of approach to the spiritual disciplines.

Energy naturally exists in a formless state until the densification process commences. The formless state of pure energy is directly relatable to the pure consciousness experienced in meditation. As energy is emitted, it begins to glow. Similarly, the glow of the light emitted is directly relatable to the self-reflexive visions and realizations caused by meditation. This glowing release of potential energy causes the vibration of energy particles which creates a sound. The subtle hum sound emitted from the vibration of energy is directly connected to the practices utilizing mantra and prayer. This sound causes a movement that naturally creates elemental clusters due to the polarization effect of sound. The clustering of energy creates pockets of identification which correlates to the path of spiritual inquiry as well as visualization. This formation of elemental clusters of energy naturally evolves into the material expression of energy. The formation of elements correlates to the ritualistic practices of a ceremony that use the elements in their invocation of the Divine. The existence of material energy slowly leads to biological evolution and eventually to self-awareness within those life forms. The formation of material energy and biological evolution is correlated to the physical postures of yoga, tai chi, and other energization exercises including some tantras. The development of society and communities of biological life forms are connected to the practices of spiritual gathering and acts of service. This is where the progression comes full circle, consciousness has created matter which is now producing its own self-awareness. There are so many techniques of spiritual discipline and each of them is a perfect reflection of the nature of subtle aspects of energy on different levels and reveal the hidden mysteries laying dormant in matter in different ways.

Using this self-awareness to inculcate consciousness through spiritual practices closes the spiraling circle of these cycles. Metaphorically, each of the stages corresponding to the development of consciousness is directly linked to a specific branch of spiritual practices.

You traverse the entire course of evolution in reverse by seeking enlightenment through practicing these limbs of spirituality. Many religions prescribe different combinations of these practices according to the mental disposition of each individual, but they are a map of the cosmos when viewed collectively.

Engaging each of the sectors of spiritual practices literally transforms the different levels of energy and corresponding realms of consciousness comprising your being into their corresponding expression of enlightened potential.

Meditation is the secret key within each of these approaches simultaneously and is naturally the most essential path to enlightenment. The root of each of these paths is the attuning of awareness to meditative level of consciousness.

However, the repetition of divine sounds called mantras will equally lead you to this same purity of consciousness. Equally so, by wholeheartedly engaging the path of self-inquiry one is naturally led to the same state. The engagement of intricate visualization techniques can equally lead one through the tiers of mind in such a way that pure consciousness is attained. The use of elements such as fire, water, and metal are common in rituals and the elemental path of performing spiritual rituals, or puja, is an equally valid path to enlightenment.

Our emotions are directly connected to our nervous system. Our nervous system is directly connected to our respiratory system. By using different breathing techniques you can direct your awareness toward consciousness as well.

There are many profound techniques which involve linking your breathing to different visualizations and mantras to lead into meditation called kriyas. The combining of different techniques of spiritual practice is particularly potent and an extremely valid path to attaining enlightenment.

The most common path of spiritual discipline in our materially identified age is yogic stretching or asana. The asanas of yoga are very powerful in multiple senses of the word. In a spiritual sense, you are taking the microcosm of your body and aligning it with the macrocosm of specific geometric shapes that correspond to the underlying laws of the cosmos. In this sense, by doing asana, you are channeling the primal energies and sacred geometries comprising the universe. When your perception becomes subtle enough this can lead to spiritual awakening through the direct perception of becoming one with the beyond.

Ultimately, this practice is primarily meant to be done to maintain bodily health as to prepare you to sit in meditation for increased periods of time. The common recommendation of most spiritual masters is 10-30 minutes of stretches a day, so you will be limber enough to sit in meditation for several hours a day.

These practices are very helpful and necessary once you reach the point in your meditations where you are sitting in meditation for hours a day. At that point, you will automatically know what stretches your body needs, but until that point, a few stretches a day is just fine.

A few other practices which are equally valid paths for attaining awakening include selfless service, feeding people, creating spiritually inspired art, studying mystic texts, practicing Feng Shui, and participating in spiritual gatherings known as satsang or sangha. Pilgrimages, certain meditative approaches to fasting, and so many other disciplines can be of explosive benefit to your evolution. The use of hand gestures known as mudras is a physical practice which can also be used to align your subtle energies and help cultivate the evolution of your presence towards pure consciousness. Mudra is a path and practice which can be effortlessly infused into your lifestyle regardless of religious affiliation or context.

No matter which path you choose to engage, from focusing solely on one technique to crafting some combination of them all, you must unavoidably take on a lifestyle of practicing some spiritual disciplines to become truly awakened.

Spiritual discipline is the force that will turn the tides of the times, both individually and for our collective evolution.

Spiritual discipline is the only path to enlightenment and therefore the only process which will lead to the liberation of total peacefulness throughout the world.

If we wish to reach the point of transforming Earth into a heavenly abode, we must transform our own selves into heavenly beings and our lives into realms of heavenly activity.

Spiritual discipline is the path, the aim, and the goal all in one. They are what will allow humanity to truly take flight. The fundamental technique and role of meditation have already been expressed, as it is the root of all other practices.

Let us now explore the healing technology of the spiritual disciplines in greater detail.

14: SONIC REHAB

We have spoken of the essence of wakeful living: formless meditation. Unfortunately, instantaneously dissolving our rational minds and human perceptions into a field of unfathomably vast light and knowingness is not always easy for hyper-conditioned adult humans who have been trained to intensively identify with thoughts, emotions, and the human body. Attaining an expansive relationship with meditation will undoubtedly take practice, but it is the most worthy dynamic to cultivate over the course of one's lifetime. If instantaneously dropping into formless meditation isn't the easiest thing for you to do at this point, don't fret as there are many helpful tools available to ease your efforts. Many of these tools were briefly outlined already, each one working with a different fundamental quality of energy. Repeating the divine name (or affirmations of sacred truth) is known as japa or the recitation of mantra. The sound of the mantra works towards evolving your awareness into pure consciousness by directly utilizing the vibrational quality of reality. The particles in the material university have vibrational tendencies which tremendously implicates how the phenomena functions as a whole.

The vibrational frequency of each particle and wave of energy, directly reflects the charge they each hold and determines how they attract, repel, or what they bond to. When this is contemplated both literally, in terms of the chemistry of the cosmos, and figuratively, in terms of the reflected patterns of consciousness implied, it is easier to perceive our lives as these subatomic ballets of energy pattern. The pattern of vibration directly correlates to how each particle functions and equally so, the patterns of our lives are correlated to the frequency of consciousness we resonate at and thereby occupy. Our entire universe's literal presentation is determined by the vibrational rates of the energy comprising what it is that we perceive. If the current combination of energy fields and particles had different rates of vibration, we would be perceiving an entirely different universe. In light of this principle, by actively determining your rate of mental vibration or by intentionally activating certain sound structures vocally, you actually reconfigure reality. So many secrets of the cosmos are connected to vibration and the correlative expression of vibration: sound.

At this point in evolution, most human beings are unable to reconstruct their subatomic energy fields using will alone; however, we actually are all capable of using our voice to create sound, in order to re-engineer our vibrational rates and perceptions of reality. By physically harnessing the vibrational power of sound you are literally rearranging your being on a physical level, which in turn transforms the mental and emotional levels of your being as well. People commonly change the music that they're listening to fit their mood. Sound therapy has become an accepted method in many professional therapeutic environments, but the sound healing techniques of the ancient mystics were meticulously mastered over thousands of years and have yet to be fully studied by the modern scientific communities.

The idea of a mantra has been completely bastardized over the last few decades, any catchphrase or slogan (even in advertising) has been labeled a mantra. There are great benefits to using mental affirmations to guide your will, but the power of a real mantra is far more vast than a catchphrase and even more vast than the mind can comprehend, by definition.

'Manas', or the root 'man' means mind and 'tra' represents the idea of control, training, or protection. So, the word mantra means mind training, mind control, or mind protection.

The meaning of these sound structures were not arbitrarily decided upon by our human minds. The most powerful of mantras were all received in deep meditation by ancient seers. They come from unimaginable realms and have properties beyond the reaches of our current understanding.

Each mantra is a multi-dimensional microcosm of pure energy. They each are living forms of the deities or cosmic qualities that they represent, literal maps of the cosmic realms they implicate, and are living light in the form of sound. The syllables vibrate as geometric patterns by design and the words they create are like sonic reflections of those geometries. Each geometry is linked with its ideal of archetype, realm, numerical system, set of divine qualities associated with those spectrums of ideals, and so much more. Each of the phrases, words, and even the seed syllables comprising true mantras are like microcosmic embodiments of the entirety of creation. They are so much more than just sounds that signify ideas, which is the level that human language traditionally functions on.

With every repetition of a true mantra you invoke pure consciousness, infusing the most subtle energetic substratum of evolutionary intelligence into your physical being on a cellular level. With every repetition of a true mantra, you are filling yourself with divine energy and reconstructing the microcosmic configuration of your human identity and literal body with the macrocosmic qualities contained within divine energy. Unspeakably profound changes occur to your mental, emotional, and physical being when you authentically practice the repetition of mantra.

Mantra transforms and elevates your entire being into echelon of the energy embodied by the sound that you are repeating. Your degree of faith in the efficacy of mantra, which is to say your degree of devotion to the divine essence which is represented by the mantra, determines the degree of charge that the sound holds as it intermingles with your being.

According the ancient Eastern mystics, we are in the densest era of consciousness, known as the Kali yuga.

During this yuga, the practice of repeating the divine name is known to be the most accessible way to awaken your enlightened nature.

Mantra is not the only path to enlightenment, but it is the smoothest road.

It can be so joyful to drop all the baggage of thought and belief and just sing to God.

It can be so pleasant and effortless to replace the static frequency of human thought, which desperately darts to and fro, with the healing sound of the divine name. When you replace your thoughts with mantra, you automatically reorient your focus towards the divine. Automatically, this shift of focus in itself is immeasurably beneficial, beyond what the mind can even perceive. As in, even if you don't know the depths of meaning contained in these few sacred syllables.

In so many senses, attention dictates reality. Where you focus your mind determines the psychological state in which you reside which shapes your perception of reality on every level. Mantra automatically brings your focus to the infinite, fills your inner vision with the glimpses of the Divine, and illuminates your life with an endless bounty of sacred occurrences.

Mantra enriches life so profoundly, especially when the mantra you are working with has been charged by the blessing of an authentic spiritual master.

You can choose any mantra you wish to repeat according to your mental disposition, but when you are given a mantra that holds the charge of someone who has actually used that very same mantra to truly reveal their own inner awakening, its power is exponentially greater. The mantra swiftly brings you through your heart into the unified field of energy, much more quickly than most paths which require you to attempt to use mere intellect and concentration to climb into a spiritual state could allow for anyone besides a master.

No matter what mantra you work with, no matter how you come by it, the regular repetition of the names of the divine is a priceless gift and joyous lifestyle that will undoubtedly uplift your awareness to the heights of pure consciousness if you stick with it.

At all costs, find the will to repeat your mantra whenever you can.

Repeating the name of God from a completely pure place within yourself, even once, is enough to attain instantaneous enlightenment.

With this in mind, imagine the exponentially compounding effect contained in hundreds, thousands, or millions of repetitions of a mantra. As you continue to work with the practice of repeating your mantra, your energy will begin overflowing to the point of automatically blessing everyone and everything you encounter. The world will begin to feel sweeter and more magical according to your will, but without effort.

In the beginning of your journey with the repetition of mantra, or japa, it is common to use a prayer necklace, known as a mala, to count your repetitions. Malas really help you stick with the mantra, especially when your mind begins to stray and tries to run away.

Ideally, you should only use your mala when you repeat your mantra as a means for deepening meditation, so you should be seated with your eyes closed and attention fixed on your third eye. You can count each repetition by moving your finger's placement from one bead to the next with each repetition. If you decide to take the traditional approach to repeating mantra using a mala, there is one bead that is clearly separate, and sometimes has a tassel attached to it, known as the Guru bead. When you reach that bead, flip the mala and change directions. You may, at that time, internally bow to Divine within or the diety presiding over the particular mantra that you are reciting.

If you chose not to use the mala in your repetition of the mantra it is known as ajapa. Ajapa is particularly helpful if you are practicing in public, carrying about your days, or going so deep into meditation that you don't want to have a physical object in your hand which can pull you back to body consciousness.

Repeating your mantra silently in your mind has a profound effect. When you repeat your mantra on a level of thought, there is less room for the mind to roam and it more easily becomes fully absorbed in the divine vibration. You will be amazed to see how quickly you can slip into meditation if you wholeheartedly focus internally on repeating a mantra while focusing on the third eye or another concentrative point or circuit.

The group chanting of mantras in sacred songs is known as kirtan. Kirtan can really amplify the energy of the mantra to amazing heights, but be careful not to make your practice solely dependent on external environments or group settings which have their inherent human dynamics that usually distract from the goal of spiritual realization.

Some traditional mantras in the yoga traditions include the name of 'RAM' and the mantra 'OM NAMAH SHIVAYA'. The most popular mantras in the Buddhist tradition are the Shakyamuni mantra, the Guru Rinpoche mantra, and the 'OM MANI PADME HUM' mantra.

If you are Christian, the name of Jesus can be taken as a mantra by repeating 'YESHU'.

Other common and extremely transformative mantras include the Mahamrityunjaya mantra, the Hare Krishna mantra, and the Gayatri Mantra.

There are millions of mantras available, some long and complex while others are short and sweet. Each has its own unique meaning and power. It is definitely worth your effort to explore the different mantras available and find the ones that fully suit your mental disposition to use in your evolution towards self mastery.

Some mantras are non-theistic while most are theistic, encapsulating the essence of a deity or divine being. You can work with many mantras if you feel inclined, but the fasted path to merging your awareness with divine consciousness is to work intensely with one mantra over your lifetime. If you are working with a mantra that represents a specific deity, you will find yourself slowly assuming the divine qualities and attributes embodied by that being until you fully identify with their enlightened nature, as it is also your own enlightened nature.

Another common aspect of the mantra practice is linking the breath with your repetitions. This link sinks the mantra's energy fully into your physical body. Riding the waves of the breath using the vehicle of the mantra is considered by many masters to be the best path to enlightenment. There are many ways to do this and levels of intricacy to the practice associated, but one of the most popular uses the mantra 'SOHAM'. Soham means 'I AM THAT' and signifies unity of the Self or Soul with the Absolute. You breathe in 'SO' and breathe out 'HAM', allowing your awareness to expand into the universe more and more entirely with each breath.

The Buddhist, non-theistic, version of the same technique involves using the mantra 'E-VAM'. 'E' signifies the ground of emptiness underlying all things and 'VAM' signifies the skillful means of engaging activity with utter mindfulness. In essence, these mantras are the same and they can both be linked to your every breath. Whether walking down the street or in the middle of a meditation session.

No matter which mantra or divine name you resonate with, linking its repetition to the breath is an amazing technique that allows your intellect and body to work in harmony as a means to expedite your attunement to pure energy and pure consciousness.

The sound that most fully encapsulates the essence of the divine is silence. It is good to set aside some time each day to simply be in silence. When we speak, our breath is made irregular and our emotions correlatively fluctuate. Extended practices of silence are particularly potent if you are truly seeking to transform your mind. Engaging in stints of silence can be tremendously cleansing and healing.

There are so many levels to the hidden magic found within the mantra. It is such a wondrous path to dance with the divine name though your days. You will find that the repetitions begin to stack up quickly.

Before you know it you will have repeated millions of mantras and will be swimming in bliss. It transforms your awareness on such a fundamental level that you will experience the residual bliss from your practice even in the most difficult of circumstances.

The repetition of mantra transforms in such a foundational way that human entrapments of ego which previously would have sent you spinning dizzily into the suffering of your own mind's making no longer effect you at all.

Each mantra is a living form of light and fills your entire being with the very light of the infinite. Other sacred sounds such as singing bowls and working with binaural beat technology has a similar effect of utilizing sound to manufacture awakened states of consciousness. The repeating of certain sutras such as the Heart Sutra can invoke similar experiences, much like how every syllable of the Hanuman Chalisa is known to be a Mahamantra.

Whichever sonic technique you use, as you work with sacred sounds, joy becomes natural.

In the wake of a sonic transformation, you would easily be able to assist with the collective human transformation.

Allow yourself to be amazed by the rehabilitation power of repeating sacred sounds.

It is such a serene way to soar.

15: SPIRITUALIZING THE MUNDANE

All of this spiritually-minded talk may seem too abstract for the modern mind. It is all too easy to put enlightenment on an unattainable pedestal within our mindsets.

In reality, God is more accessible than the ego will ever be willing to accept. Divinity is the foundation of the formation of reality. It is each building block comprising everything that any of us have ever experienced. There is nothing outside the consciousness which sparked the cycles within creation. It is that very same Universal intelligence which breathes our very breath.

We all must learn to regularize spirituality into our identity and existence. We must come to normalize the loftiest realizations as our very own original nature.

To do so, it will require each of us to flood our lives with elements of Divine realms, mandalas of spiritual activity. We must infuse the brilliance of the Divine into our everyday habits and patterns of activity.

Without making too big of a deal about it, we have to regularize the aspects of spiritual discipline into our seemingly mundane routines. By contemplating life's largest questions regularly, you bring the scope of your mind out of the mundane and into the spiritual, even when you are performing the most simplistic of tasks. Try to see the macrocosm whilst functioning in the microcosm. Self-inquiry is an ever-available and invisible doorway to elevating consciousness. Focusing on the Divine and continually contemplating the truth can easily be anchored into your day to day activities as a means of spiritualizing your world view. Bring your awareness of the infinite level of mind into your human, function-oriented, limited mind.

This normalization process is how we will seamlessly integrate our compassionate potential into the arenas of society's construction. This normalization process is how we come to embody our highest archetypical potential. You become your higher self by integrating the spark of loving presence into every crevasse of your existence, every moment you witness. Tenderly massage your divinity into the shadowy corners of your humanness.

You don't have to run away from society to become spiritual. You don't have to renounce human activities to grow into your enlightened potential. Slowly and with love, your spiritual disciplines will naturally increase if you truly tend to them with care. With minimal strain, a few minutes of meditative practice each day can rapidly evolve into a few hours each day. You don't have to become a monk, or a sadhu, to grow into the kind of person who practices daily spiritual disciplines. Spiritual discipline is known as sadhana. Those who practice sadhana are known as sadhikas. You don't have to be a sadhu to be a sadhika.

You can be the Buddha just as you are, for your true nature is already an embodiment of Buddha nature.

Begin by transforming little habits.

Inch by inch, take your mundane activity into the sphere of Buddha activity. A great place to start is on the level of mind. Integrate spiritual self inquiry into your common cycles in the spheres of your inner contemplation. Without changing any of your literal, physical habits you can begin to shift your mental habits.

Remind yourself regularly of the most profound spiritual insights you've ever conceived of and the highest visions your inner sights have yet to glimpse. Think deeply about what those experiences really mean and how those truths inform your waking, subjective, human awarenesses true nature.

Train your mind to remember the Divine.

It helps greatly to study the spiritual scriptures of the different spiritual masters from the many blessed traditions worldwide, at least until the stream of your thoughts are fixed on higher truths without your effort.

Slowly decrease the activities that you know in your intuitive clarity are actually negative influences for you. Be brutally honest with yourself. What habits can you replace with new habits that are more in alignment with your intentions for self-mastery?

We all feed our minds a large amount of delusion and illusory phenomena just by engaging modern culture. Until you maintain absolute clarity, it will be helpful to limit your exposure to worldly oriented sensory perceptions. Eventually you will able to maintain inner wakefulness regardless of what your outward attention is focused on, but it takes practice. Keeping a generally inward-turned focus and withdrawing your attention from the material world is known as pratyahara, and is a very helpful practice.

If this doesn't fit your ideals for your lifestyle, it isn't a problem. As you engage other spiritual disciplines, your detachment from the material world will naturally increase in due time.

A great way to expedite that process is through different breathing techniques. They each bring your awareness to a very subtle state, but in different fashions according to the method.

One popular technique is known as alternate breathing. In a seated position with your right hand's fingers fully extended, bring your middle and pointer fingers to your palm. Now push your thumb gently against your nose to close your right nostril and fully exhale out of your left nostril. After a pause, inhale through your left nostril while still covering your right. Once you have fully inhaled, as you are briefly pausing, switch to gently pushing your left nostril closed with your extended pinky and ring fingers. Exhale fully out of your right nostril and pause.

Next inhale, use just your right nostril and repeat this cycle of switching back and forth between the nostrils for a few minutes.

This practice calms your nervous system, slows your thoughts, and helps align the hemispheres of your brain.

It is a simple technique that can invoke a calm and spiritual state upon command with great ease.

There are many other helpful examples of breathing techniques, such as bastrika, that may be worth investigating if this is a path that resonates with you.

The paths of relating to the Divine are many and varied, but the more you can naturalize their presence in your life the more you will find yourself in the subliminal sacredness that emerges through each moment.

Prayer is a practice that has been stigmatized in our culture. With the recognition of Universal intelligence as fundamental to creation, the idea of using your thoughts to interweave your mind in the field of collective consciousness through prayer becomes much more natural and intellectually graspable.

Every thought is a prayer, most people just don't realize it.

Prayer doesn't have to be done from a place of ego.

You don't have to ask for anything to pray. Prayer isn't about getting a pet pony or a job promotion, it is about attuning your limited mind to the infinite level of mind.

In many senses, mantra is prayer.

In another sense, by contemplating the abstract and philosophical truths of reality, you are praying.

Many atheists pray all the time without realizing it. Prayer is simply any God-centric or high-minded thought. When you use your will and awareness to connect to the formless luminosity within, you are actively engaging your own highest nature. When you pray or focus on the Divine, it is actually God that is focusing on you.

By repeating a name of God or focusing on God, your prayers are automatically answered on a deeper level than your rational mind can comprehend because the summation of your thoughts on a subconscious level is automatically being woven into the web of the Divine's awareness of your consciousness when you pray.

The more you consume your thoughts with focus on the Divine, the more you become one with the Divine.

This can be done throughout your days in endless ways: while eating, sleeping, working or making love.

There needn't be a break in your Divine-attunement, so long as you can still function properly in your life.

Most people want to pretend that our awarenesses are insular and isolated. The more you investigate the nature of the mind, the more you will discover that this simply isn't the case.

If you are ever blessed enough to meet an enlightened being, you will come to witness how truly shared our spheres of mind are.

Fasting is another powerful spiritual practice, but it is not a spiritual end unto itself. This practice can help bring subtly to your awareness, but you must be careful when entering such dangerous waters. It is best to fast in delicate moderation. It can be used to recenter your awareness, but fasting cannot lead you to enlightenment on its own, only in combination with other practices.

Think about how many people die of starvation without achieving enlightenment. Its value is only in correlation to your inner aspiration.

The truest fasting is not fasting at all. The essence of this notion is best represented through a tale about the founder of Hassidic Judaism, named the Baal Shem Tov. He once brought a week's worth of bread into a locked temple to pray. When the week was up, his attendant came to bring him out of seclusion and found the entire week's worth of bread still sitting untouched and the Baal Shem Tov had absolutely no clue because he was so absorbed in the Divine that he didn't even noticed that he hadn't eaten.

This is true fasting, not fasting at all.

Another profound spiritual practice that can easily be taken on is eating only vegetarian food.

This isn't required to spiritualize your life, but it is a simple way to act out of compassion for sentient beings. Even if you do not take this practice on full time, it is helpful to do so during spiritual retreats specifically.

Whether or not you become vegetarian isn't going to cause you to attain enlightenment nor will it prevent you from attainment. However, it helps increase your spiritual sensitivity. By not taking on the energy and emotions of another living being, you can more easily align your own mind and your own emotions with your higher potential.

Any expression of compassion that you can take on is of service to all sentient beings and will in turn bless your spiritual path. Any time you offer the merit of your sadhana to the collective well-being, it will in turn bless your path exponentially.

Any attempt of serving humanity is a service to your own spiritual growth.

Gathering with like-minded individuals and practicing any form of spiritual discipline is a profound form of serving the collective known as sating or sangha.

In a sense, it is also a revolutionary act to do so.

Your revolutions don't have to be marches and petitions, but the simple act of naturalizing spirituality is one of the most revolutionary things you can do in a world that is so full of materialism, pain, and suffering.

The more you can integrate the different activities of spirituality into your mundane routines, the more you will revolutionize the world at large.

Every act may seem small, but the collection of actions taken over just one lifetime add up to a mountain of divinity before you know it.

16: FEAST OF FORM

As you rise into a lifestyle of regular spiritual discipline and begin to experience authentic mystical revelation, you will naturally find yourself reaching a few crossroads. The journey of evolving into regularly having out-of-body experiences doesn't make your body go away by any means.

Just as hunger comes and goes, so too does sexual desire. As you detach from the gripping mentality of the material realm as fixed or solid you may witness your sexual desires spontaneously slip away into the etheric nothingness.

Just as suddenly desire can once again rear its entrancing head and so you may at times find yourself even more consumed by your passions than before you started working with subtle energy and spiritual self-effort. This will likely continue to happen in waves as you move into fully embodying pure awareness.

Sexual desire is the most fickle of energies to navigate and delicately difficult of aspects to traverse on the journey of spiritual awakening. This level of overwhelming desire may likely melt away at a certain point if you continue wholeheartedly on the path of sadhana, but it isn't going to be helpful to engage the charade of having already transcended your desires if you are really just repressing them.

The power of your cravings can jump out and devour you if your spiritual ego isn't kept in check. This is why there are so many examples of half-baked spiritual teachers (and even many mostly baked ones) that turn to a destructive level of sexual transgression once they've been put in a position of power.

Sexuality is something that is functioning in our bodies on a chemical level. For the entire course of human history, our urge to reproduce was fundamental to the survival of our species. Now, for the majority of the circumstances on this overpopulated planet, sexuality exists primarily for self-indulgence. There are so many joyful reasons to engage desire, but there are also many reasons why the traditional teachings of spiritual discipline encourage that we mostly don't.

On the most basic level, desire is usually a distraction that prevents our our minds from maintaining attunement to that ultimate reality which is beyond form. If you are truly attempting to recondition your mental identification with separateness, the emotionally activating embrace of sexual desire can be an intensely distracting force. It is for this reason that monks have traditionally kept vows of celibacy.

Their vows are not made because sex is inherently wrong by any means, but because for the student of self-mastery it can be extremely distracting from cosmic consciousness.

Also, if you are truly reaching meditative states of cosmic proportion, the subtle bliss of the divine is infinitely more orgasmic than the physical touch could ever be on its own. If you think sex is more pleasurable than meditation, you haven't reached the heights of meditation's potential. Although to be fair, most people don't start the path of meditation at such a level where they could recognize this truth and therefore never aspire longingly enough to know it as true.

The irony is that at the beginning of the spiritual path you are likely not having many meditation experiences that are more orgasmic than the human touch, so you are more inclined to continue engaging your sexual desires, but that is actually when isolating from the dynamics of dualistic passions is the most helpful. Likewise for the true master, their pose of union with the Divine is unshakeable, so it doesn't matter as much whether or not they engage sexually from the viewpoint of whether or not it effects true wakefulness, but at that point of meditative mastery the desire often doesn't exist in the same manner. Most masters just avoid the dynamic as it often confuses the minds of their students. It is a tricky paradox of timing that we all must reconcile on the spiritual path.

Engaging with someone sexually causes an unseen link between the given partners fields of energy and consciousness for several months. Once you engage with someone sexually, you share karmic impressions for a stretch of time that is determined by your degree of attachment and love, whether or not you are in continued physical contact with that person. This is the importance of being extremely mindful of who you engage with sexually.

You are entrusting your storehouse of spiritual energy to whomever you jump in bed with, whether you realize it or not. This is why, if you are going to continue to engage your sexuality while attempting to attain enlightenment, it is always helpful to have just one partner at a time and to give yourself a stretch of energetic regeneration and self-reflection between each partner.

If you are fully serious about enlightenment, it is best to temporarily avoid engaging your sexual desires completely, at least until you have stabilized in an awakened state. We must acknowledge how the different saints and buddhas have have actually lived if we truly wish to become awakened as they have and are. However, we must also be practical in acknowledging the fact that we are living in a different era of culture and society than the majority of historical seekers.

It is important to be honest about what degree of wakefulness you are actually attempting to achieve, where on the path you actually are currently, and what lifestyle is actually most advantageous to you.

If you are fully committed to enlightenment then it is important to know the role of celibacy outside the dualistic dichotomy of "right and wrong". Celibacy is not right or wrong, it is a matter of energy control.

Your subtle energy is called shakti, which is the substratum of the cosmos and embodiment of the Divine Mother microcosmically We all have a storehouse of this subtle energy that becomes active within us as we spiritually awaken. As your wakefulness increases, this energy slowly replaces each cell of your material body with pure light until your physical body literally vibrates at a different frequency.

The increase of the degree to which you have personally awakened the shakti within is what gives you the ability to enter into cosmic states of meditative consciousness upon command.

You have to totally close all the doors and windows of your being which causes you to lose your storehouse of subtle energy if you wish to contain this enlightened experience and fully stabilize as a awakened being. Once you hit a certain threshold of saturation in wakefulness, there is nothing that can deplete your storehouse any longer because you will have consciously forged an unbreakable bond to the infinite.

If you are engaging in a time of heightened spiritual discipline like a retreat or are establishing a new routine of deeper sadhana, it is extremely helpful to practice temporary periods of celibacy. This doesn't mean you have to take a vow, become a monk, or become an asexual for life. It is helpful to work with restraint while you are vital and can conjure a great degree of disciplined aspiration towards self-mastery.

In fact, this type of energy control actually resets your vitality and youthfulness in many mind-blowing ways. So, even if you are not specifically on a retreat of spiritual discipline, it is spiritually advantageous to simply regulate your desires (whatever that means relative to you).

The nature of desire is to grow endlessly.

This is why it is ideal for most modern individuals to simply put a limit on sexual engagement instead of trying to shut it out completely.

Although limited engagements of celibacy can be essential for part of the spiritual path, the path of engaging a committed relationship can actually cause some of the most potent spiritual work available during human incarnation to occur. A truly committed partnership is one of the fastest evolutionary paths of self-work. Having a partner who is also on the path of spiritual self-effort especially can be one of the most profound mirrors in reflecting one's true state and helping with one's development.

If you are on the path of authentically seeking enlightenment and are on the path of engaging your sexuality, it is important to turn that part of your life into a practice. That can include everything from simply being more mindful during the ritual of lovemaking to the extremes of some pretty esoteric tantric techniques that involve breathing techniques, visualizations, mantras, and so many more profoundly liberating techniques being brought into that intimate environment which brings the sexual experience to new heights.

On the basic level of sexual tantra, you should be aware that subtle energy is moving through your physical being at all times, even while engaging in this very worldly act. Try to maintain the mental attitude that you are not two separate physical beings, but one being expressed through cooperative parts of the same whole.

This level of awareness can be easily cultivated by attempting to maintain awareness of your third eye while engaging the physical process, as well as by feeling overwhelming love in your heart for your partner and all of creation.

If you are aware of the pathways of subtle energy in the body then you can also actively visualize the energy rising up the core of your being into the third eye or through the crown of your head as you engage in this ritual of passion. The more levels of focal points you can attune to throughout the process, the better it will serve the meditative potential of the experience as the energy increases.

Acknowledging the mantra as an ultimate expression of spiritual energy, it is especially helpful to repeat a mantra while engaging intimately. This can be done mentally or out loud by either individual, but is more effective if both partners are mentally or vocally engaging in corresponding mantra repetition.

You can even use your minds and wills to visualize infusing mantras of light into each other's physical beings.

The most advanced tantric monks of Vajrayana Buddhism are carefully guided into these types of practices with a partner in a corresponding lineage chosen by their guru.

They take on extremely advanced visualization rituals in order to elevate this tantric process. These rituals include maintaining mantras while visualizing copulating deities in a complex mandala, or sacred geometric grid.

This advanced level of technique is designed to lead both partners to an enlightened state.

It is important to keep in mind that intertwining your increased sensitivity to someone else's ego and karmic path can become a very narrow and slippery journey. Emotions can cause one to quickly go insane or at least lose the peace of mind needed to meditate. Attachment derived from sexuality can easily make one or both partners turn into an egomaniac before they even realize it. Working with this type of energy can also create a craving for more and more sexual partners to satisfy the unending appetite which is even further expanded by the spiritual energy.

This is why the sexual techniques of tantra are traditionally always met with an equal amount of mind training in regards to emptiness and maintaining detachment.

If you are on the tantric path, your desire becomes your ritual and offering. Whether you are cooking, cleaning, or making love, it should become a ritualistic feast of form.

It is probably best to leave this level of tantra to those with proper training and guidance.

Most of the true masters maintain celibacy even after attaining total enlightenment.

Not because they need to for energy regulation, but because people often misinterpret their activity. In many cases, they simply transcend sexual desires altogether.

No matter what form of the spiritual path you choose to walk, whether engaging your sexual desires mindfully or mindfully detaching from those impulses, it is important to set natural limitations for your desires in all spheres of your life.

Sometimes having sex will just be having sex.

Maybe, from time to time, you will make love for days on end and when that is over your desire will subside for a while, and you can simply return to a time of being more dialed in to meditation practice and spiritual self-efforts.

It all comes in waves.

Sometimes you will feel too sensitive and imbalanced after attempting periods of celibacy to such a point where you just feel you have to masturbate. There is no problem with doing whatever you have to do to be true to yourself and your path, but it is important to know how working with your sexuality can elevate or lower your level of awareness. That is all. No judgments of approach or moral absolutes about it.

However you choose to deal with these impulses, you can't avoid their existence.

Make your approach your path.

Everything you do becomes the path when you set your intentions on awakening.

Make each aspect of your lifestyle a means for heightening intentionality.

If you do so, no matter what lifestyle you lead, you will become spiritually fulfilled and be able to properly serve humanity in its arc of collective awakening.

17: SACRAMENTAL SADHANA

No aspect of life can be excluded in the quest for enlightenment. Everything you do, say, believe and consume directly effects your consciousness. Clarity and precision of mind are some of your greatest allies available for transcending the mind itself. The traditional teachings of many spiritual traditions advise to avoid mind-altering substances, but in the modern world, almost everyone has a regular relationship with some chemical substance or another. Whether you drink tea, soda, or liquor, your consciousness is going to be effected accordingly. This doesn't have to be a problem spiritually, but it is another circumstance where the tantric approach of working with the illusion as a vehicle for awakening is required. Tantra is far more than ritualistic sex. True tantra is any practice that allows you to transform your perception of phenomena as you know it, using the constructs of the experience itself as the means for transcending delusion.

What is most important on the spiritual path is not copying the rule book, getting the most merit badges, or giving up all your habits, but turning every aspect of your life into your practice. This requires many transformations of approach including turning your consumptive patterns into sacramental ceremonies. Through intentionally reconstructing your habits as to fully make each action into a divine offering, the way you identify with each aspect of your life will naturally evolve accordingly.

You will find that fixations of habit and unsustainable choices naturally melt away in the blossoming of your inner attunement.

Not all substances effect our awareness equally. It is very difficult to make drugs like PCP or meth truly serve your spiritual progress or meditation practice except in the soul searching that follows the come down. Perhaps it is possible to use these as sacraments, but for the most part they are going to be more addictive and delusion inspiring than one can control or utilize evolutionarily.

The most common mind-altering substance used in our society is alcohol. Alcohol has some spiritual possibility, at least more than the chemicals previously mentioned, but is still very difficult to direct towards completely sacramental use. By design, alcohol makes you unaware of how intoxicated you are. However, when used in moderation and brought into ceremony, alcohol has actually been effectively used as a sacrament in many cultures including certain lineages of Buddhism, Christianity, and Judaism. All in all, if you're truly serious about awakening through the meditation path it is best to at least wait to start drinking each day until after you've done your daily meditation practice. However, many tantric Buddhists would beg to differ.

The most universally common sacramental substance, which is used by Shiva worshippers and Rastafarians alike, is cannabis. Cannabis naturally draws your focus inward and, when used properly, can help invoke a meditative state. It can, however, also be rather disorienting and cause a lose of clarity, which is extremely important on the spiritual path. If you are using cannabis wholeheartedly with the intention of focusing on the Divine, then it can be a very helpful tool and can be easily worked with sacramentally in your sadhana.

It is difficult to use cannabis to achieve completely unbroken states of wakefulness, but it can be very good for relaxing the mind into temporary meditation states, opening the heart to greater compassion and healing the body in so many capacities.

If you smoke cannabis then it will effect the regulation of your breathing. It all causes your mind to crave more after a few hours, so it is only really helpful if you are meditating for less than three or four hours a day. Nonetheless, cannabis is such a helpful tool, much like training wheels, for transcending the mind in meditation. Creating edible forms of cannabis can help in avoiding common drawbacks and prolonging the benefit of the sacrament. Cannabis is a profound substance when used for establishing and expanding your initial practice, but after some time you may find it to be a hindrance to maintaining meditation states for extremely extended periods of time.

The primary and most explosively inspiring forms of sacrament on the spiritual path are the different psychedelics. Psychedelics open your mind and vision to layers upon layers of inner vision and can lead the practitioner to a truly rapid spiritual awakening.

This is the fastest, and therefore the most dangerous, path to realization. Psychedelics allow you to slip into yogic states of consciousness effortlessly, but they only last as long as the substance lasts. They give you a taste of the Divine's royal banquet, but then quickly toss you back out on the streets.

If psychedelics are over-indulged in, there is a real risk of developing psychosis as the line between fantasy and reality becomes very blurred. The difference between using drugs and utilizing sacrament is a fine line. Many people use psychedelics, but never achieve spiritual awakening because they are not intentionalized in their use as sacrament. The difference is all about intention, attention, set, and setting.

Your intention for using psychedelics should always be for assisting your evolution, not just to party and feel groovy. Your attention directs your reality, so your focus will determine the outcome of your experience. It is very important to focus on the inner realms, your personal growth, and seeking Divine truths if you are going to engage such a risky path as using psychedelic substances.

If you treat the experience as a spiritual experience then the experience will grant you a sense of spirituality and bring you to profound visions. This means it is best to take psychedelic sacrament in a quiet place with space to meditate comfortably, not at a festival or party. "Set and setting" is a common phrase in the psychedelic communities which means that your experience is dependent on what you are consciously consuming and where you are consuming it.

This path is definitely not recommended for everyone, but if you choose to go down this path make sure to keep your vision true and maintain focus on seeking.

Each psychedelic will effect your path to inner vision differently according to the nature of the substance. Mushrooms are a dissociative drug. They will break down your perceptions and their correlating conceptions. This can be very helpful for freeing you from your boxes of belief, but be very careful where and how rapidly you break down your world view through dissociations. Mushrooms are liable to melt all sense of clarity which can cause doubt and greater confusion if not handled reverently and delicately.

It is also important to not dissociate your mind so often that you lose your ability to properly associate who needed and function in your day to day life. You will know when you are dancing that line. It is an easy line to cross with mushrooms, but in the same sense, it is easy to transcend the mind with mushrooms when used sacramentally. So they definitely shouldn't be labeled as spiritually irrelevant.

Ecstasy is a less inherently spiritual substance compared to mushrooms, but it can fill you with Divine love and help lead into meditation states if used as a sacrament. Usually it is used merely to increase your pleasure, sensuality, desire, attachment while used as a party drug. Its up to you how you use it or not. MDMA can have a very therapeutic benefit when done properly and is very helpful if used in combination with meditation. Most people do not use ecstasy or sassafras in this way, just as a way to party. If you do walk down this path, stay very hydrated, give yourself a rest day afterward to recover, and do not use them too frequently as they can easily cause tremendous brain damage.

While mushrooms dissociate, LSD is all about connectivity and heightened association. It will cause your mind to make profound connections of all the dots, even when there actually isn't as much of a connection as you would like to think. LSD can be one of the most spiritually uplifting substances when used sacramentally, but it can also cause the mind to create some of the greatest leaps of assumption, false beliefs, and out right delusions.

LSD is a sacrament that is very naturally inclined towards assisting in spiritual awakening, but definitely take your experiences with a grain of salt. It doesn't break down your ego, it inflates it and to cosmic proportions. LSD has more extended peaks and stretches of visionary insight than some of the other psychedelics so overall it is very helpful for learning the terrain of the spiritual and meditative realms of consciousness.

It is important to tread lightly, but acid can give you incredible spiritual insight, inspiration, and cause a rapidly increased rate of spiritual growth when directed properly.

Mescaline also has an inherently spiritual leaning and is much more grounding by nature than the experience of LSD. Due to its connection to the plant world and the shamanic traditions, mescaline can be the safest route of psychedelic journeying. It is ideal to use it under the guidance of a true shaman, but overall is definitely the most integrated psychedelic with the actual mysticism underlying reality and has the least amount of negative repercussions on the body.

DMT is a fast and furious form of psychedelic sacrament. It lasts only fifteen to twenty-five minutes yet provides the full range of non-ordinary perceptual experience that is normally stretched out over many hours with other psychedelics. It is advisable to only use this psychedelic sacrament once you have experience with other sacraments so that you can handle this expedited version of the journey. DMT is naturally produced in your brain when dreaming, as you are born, and as you are dying, so it is much like a waking dream state or a lucid dream that is entered while waking. Your subconscious will direct the visions within this experience so, again, it is also best to use in combination with meditation.

Ketamine has highly dissociative qualities so be sure you are in a comfortable environment while engaging this substance and, again, making it a sacrament is best while being consumed.

A much safer and more subtle form of sacrament is the sound technology of binaural beats. Binaural beats are a form of sound technology that uses the combination of two tones to create a third tone that vibrates at a rate which can automatically produce meditation brain waves known as theta waves. If you entrain your mind by listening to binaural beats for more than about ten minutes at a time, they will automatically cause meditation-like experiences to occur. When used in combination with the discipline of meditation, the awareness associated with binaural beats become much like that of psychedelics. This is a great example of a safer and more subtle sacrament, but even binaural beats can't be relied on as the sole source of your liberation.

Each of these chemical compounds leaves an edge to your awareness, more so than spiritual disciplines done in sobriety unto themselves do, and therefore they leave a sort of psychic residue. They can cause fear and often times confusion, so be extremely careful even if you reach states of spiritual ecstasy using these substances. They are authentic and a blessing for humanity's evolution, but be cautious and don't believe everything you think or even envision.

If you do partake of this path, it is advantageous to try your best to undo the residual confusion caused by psychedelics through regularizing the same visionary states that you achieve through psychedelics without chemical influence. These chemicals can open the door to Divine states of consciousness when used properly, but you must then learn to meditate and use other spiritual disciplines to unlock those same doors with your will alone after having glimpsed these levels of mind through psychedelics.

Using sacrament is a very dangerous path. If you have a history of mental instability, it is not the path for you.

It is a path best matched with intense study of the spiritual teachings and an even more intense commitment to daily spiritual disciplines.

Even if you do choose to engage the sacramental path of psychedelics, you will eventually have to walk the path without them because they are not something that can be done daily as a replacement for discipline. They are meant to bring you into the stream of yogic consciousness, but you must learn to swim if you do not wish to drown or live solely on the shore.

You will reach a point where sacrament becomes unwanted. More so, you will reach a point where sobriety is wholly valued. With the insight and vision derived from your deepest dives into the use of sacraments, you will naturally reach the point of being able to integrate these spiritual states into your walking and waking states.

The real magic of sacrament isn't just the moment of epiphany at the peak of the trip, but the ability to weave that perpetually awe-inspiring experience of epiphany into every facet and moment of your normal awareness.

Many well-intending beings have gone over the edge with this path and it is for that reason that most spiritual teachers do not accept psychedelics as an appropriate part of the path.

You must use your will in combination with whatever path you choose to properly undertake the journey to enlightenment.

At the core, only you can bring yourself to the point of embodying your spiritual potential fully.

No shaman, sacrament, or ceremony can do the work for you, but they can open the door.

18: EVERYDAY DIVINITY

Cultivating Heaven on Earth is not a once a weekend event nor something to be left for special retreats. The dimensionless luminosity of the transcendental essence underlying all things is available in each moment.

To fully transform our broken world, we have to completely permeate our lives with techniques and tactics which have been proven to invoke our sublimated divinity every single day.

To live in the spirit of the wisdom of the absolute we must not only cultivate an understanding of the Divine presence, but also learn to apply that understanding to every iota of each arena of our life styles. This application process can be seen as the development of what is known as upaya, or having mindful precision in the use of skillful means. Upaya is the essence of tantra. Infusing the recognition of the ever-present Divine nature with the practical wisdom needed to bring it into form is upaya.

Whether you are meditating, chopping vegetables, or vacuuming your floor: there is always the potential of doing every activity in an enlightened manner and therefore, there is always an opportunity to bring tantra, ceremony, ritual, or some general sense of cosmic dignity into your approach.

The traditional boundaries held between what is religious and secular do not apply to the truth of upaya, you can conceivably drink a beer or make love in just as enlightened of a manner as you can meditate or practice breathing techniques.

No matter what you are doing, if it is done from a state of wakefulness you will be infusing luminosity into that activity. You will eventually go from intellectually identifying as a buddha to literally seeing yourself as a being of made golden light and living in your own buddha-mandala realm.

The path of working with ego, identification, and appropriately reaching a point of acknowledging yourself as truly awakened can be very tricky. As long as you believe your ego identity and the phenomena comprising time-space to be solidly real notions, you are still deeply submerged in self-deception.

The recognition of the emptiness underlying phenomena is absolutely necessary to properly engage this path of seeing through illusion, especially when performing the daily routines which can make us feel all-too-human. With this recognition of emptiness held close, you can begin to cultivate the awareness of yourself as a Divine being living in a sacred realm.

Infinite microcosms are emanating from your being, meaning that there are endless "you's" emerging from your every breath, your every step, your every pore. On an energy level subtle realms are rippling forth, being emanated all around you, constantly. Little imprints of you, which slightly fluctuate in design according to what level of energy and awareness you are operating from, are manifesting manifesting subtly from moment to moment.

If you repeat a mantra you are not just worshipping Krishna, Shiva, or Padmasambhava, but you are actually becoming them through a astral body transmission technology. All of your subtle emanations begin to align with the energy fields of those identities.

You could visualize or imagine these subtle-energetic emanations as a part of your perception, but the constant engagement of spiritual disciplines such as japa and meditation will automatically produce the awareness of these perceptions of emanations over time. It is one thing to imagine yourself as a Divine being while doing everyday activities, but it is another thing to practice the techniques which are actualizing the essence of this process in infinitely profound and mysterious ways.

Any authentic spiritual practice one engages in literally infuses Divine awareness and light into the material sphere. This is the core purpose underlying the act of any ritual. You are inculcating higher expressions of potentiality by harmonizing your frequency with the infinitely present and unshakable frequency of the Divine as a means to bring the higher realms into and through the literal situations of your present experience in this physical realm.

When you use your will to chant mantra in a fire or water ceremony, you are actually invoking the deity embodied by the sacred syllables and infusing their literal light into those elements which, in turn, is also integrated into your environment. This is the invisible tale of ceremony that is being told to those who are aware of what can be known as 'astral body technology'.

Every picture of a Divine being, when acknowledged with reverence, is a vehicle for transmitting astral light-bodies into the physical world. Every time you think of a Divine being with reverence, you are actually calling upon the many subtle energetic or astral bodies of that being to come to you and infuse your illusion of individual being with their connection to the universal light and essence.

The joy and inner peace you experience when performing a ritual, when you pray, or bow to a shrine, is actually the subtle energy of the enlightened essence literally coming to you through the entities connected to that specific altar. Whether bowing to a shrine, a statue, a picture of a Divine being, or simply internally bowing to your conception of cosmic consciousness or an enlightened being in your mind's eye, the effect is the same. The energy of the Divine is literally imbued into your reality through acts such as these and any of the wholly mystic order, especially meditation. Yet it is your duty as an awakening seeker to find the portals in each circumstance you encounter which allow for the inner mysticism and magic to come forth and flourish. You have to actively bring the Divine into the everyday.

Rituals such as puja can be performed anywhere, at any time. There are five ingredients that are present in all puja and seem to translate as the universally core ingredients of all rituals throughout different cultures. Those five ingredients are dhoop, dheep, pushpa, mantra, and prasad. Dhoop means incense, but this can be represented in your ceremonial endeavors with any enjoyable smell. Dheep means light, like from the use of a candle or a fire, but the presence of anything representing the Divine light works. That can mean anything from using a flashlight to visualizing the light from within if you do not have external props present for your ceremony. Any practices done externally can also be done internally (mentally) to great effect. Pushpa means flowers, but any Divine offering representing the living essence of the natural world will work just fine. A picture of a flower or a crystal could work, the energy from these offerings still invokes the same eternal qualities associated with this aspect of ritual. Mantra means the name of the Divine, but in general this category of puja can be accounted for in your rituals through invocation of the Divine through any language model that is most natural to you. This can include scriptural recitation, prayer, hymnal, kirtan, japa, or even silence. The final of the five aspects of puja is known as prasad which is an offering to the Divine that is usually food.

When you ceremonial incorporate these universal elements into any given situation, you create a ritual out of the moment which is proportionally manifesting a Divine realm out of a previously human one.

There is a common practice of yogic ritual called aarti. Aarti involves the clockwise rotation of a flame before images of the Divine in combination with the recitation of mantra. To the untrained eye, this may seem like a strange performance. To the trained eye, this is a profound way to invoke Divine energies. When you perform a ritual to a statue of the Divine, you are not worshipping that literal statue or murti, but the indwelling essence as embodied by the deity represented through the statue. True idol worship is no idol worship at all, just a means of relating the limited mind to the unlimited potential of God.

This process allows you to slowly move towards embodying and identifying with that divinity yourself.

Similarly, performing a ceremony with a Shiva lingam does not mean worshipping a stone or phallic image, it is worshipping the infinite through the finite as represented by this ovoid shape which is beginningless and endless.

There are hidden and subtle practices of harmonization and identification that can be integrated into everything we do. Every single aspect of your day can become so much more than you being just a biological creature carrying out its necessary functions. Your activity can easily be elevated to the realm of divinity with a simple shift of perception.

Every tantric ceremony, as well as mundane activities that are done with a focus on the Divine, literally transforms your realm into a consciously embodied extension of the realm inhabited by your chosen deity of worship.

This is one of the secrets of working with astral body technologies. By installing an altar or participating in a ceremony you are literally acting in the live theatre of the Divine form. Through regularly engaging spiritual disciplines and the ceremonialization of all activities in your life, you play the role of the higher archetype of Self until those qualities are fully transmitted to your individual being and lead to eventually identifying with the macrocosm of enlightened consciousness more so than the microcosm of the body which it inhabits. The act of performing spiritual practices is the path of replicating Divine realms as a means of the altering identification.

Just like when you begin to feel the emotions of a character while watching an engrossing movie or a play, which at times even causes physical reactions to occur as if you were the character themselves, this ritualization path of awakening creates the same osmosis of identification.

Ritual is the ultimate expression of magical realism.

Our world is a multi-dimensional stage in which we perform the plays of our own imagining. The story you live, and in turn the story you tell is determined by the character you are choosing to manifest through each of the daily actions and inner states that comprise your life.

You don't have to engage in complex visualization tantras or rituals to be living with compassion, which is the ultimate ritual for bringing Heaven to Earth. By simply acting from compassion you are bringing a bodhisattva realm into the material world.

By being wakeful you become an embodiment of Buddha Nature. By practicing Divine rituals, you become the Divine itself. The ritualization of everyday activity is skillful means, upaya.

This can be exemplified by being more present while you wash the dishes, but it could also mean literally practicing rituals such as puja or aarti.

The approaches and applications of upaya are limitless, but whichever form you engage it is helpful to acknowledge that there is more to this moment than what meets the eye.

In fact, by performing spiritual activities and engaging in spiritual disciplines, you are not only focusing on higher realms and beings, but on a subtle and often unseeable level these realms are literally being installed into your form and the realms you cultivate through your life.

Ritualistically and ceremonially enriching your everyday experience isn't limited to one religion or another.

Every single religious path's tools and terminologies can be used as a mystic gateway to bring the Divine into the drudgery of day to day life. This is the beauty of the age of the Triadic Singularity.

You are not limited to the techniques or practices of any one religion. You do not have to start a new religion to bring the ideals of yoga into an Abrahamic religions. You do not have to prevent yourself from bringing a devotion to Allah into your practice of Buddhism. All paths are intertwined just as reality's scintillating tapestry of phenomena are interwoven.

None of the recent advancements of spiritual culture have actually been new approaches at all. All of the recently popularized spiritual teachers and practices have constructed fusions of pre-existent religious practices. They have done so to make these practices more accessible and normalized for our modern mindsets, which often resist the formality of religious antiquity.

In reality, you don't need to pay anyone to teach you how to integrate these practices into your heart and mind and days. You can sit down with the wisdom of the scriptures from around the world and weave a tapestry of your own design.

You don't have to join a religion or spiritual community to slowly begin integrating profound spiritual techniques and rituals into the activities and beliefs that wholeheartedly feel authentic to you based on your life path and your unique constitution.

You may draw inspiration from all the different world religions and spiritual paths, just one, or none at all. Nothing should stop you from elevating the culture of activity within your lifestyle in whatever ways feel most real for you.

What is most important is not which practices you engage, but that you engage them.

The momentum required to bring Heaven to Earth is infinite, so your spiritual self-effort must be continuous (or at least become a daily habit). Your storehouse and momentum of development towards subtle energetic embodiment is reset every day that you don't invoke subtle energy through meditation and spiritual practices.

Meditate every single day and you will come to know God.

If you truly wish to attain enlightenment in this lifetime and to bring Heaven to Earth, you must bring the revitalizing touch of the Divine presence into every single day of the rest of your life.

19: THE HIGHER SELF

There are many tools on the spiritual path which can help you attain awakening, but you still must use your will to wield those tools. Many great masters have walked the path before these forms of us, yet no one can truly walk the path for us in this life. The examples of the lives of spiritual masters can serve as directive guidance for us as we learn to climb to the heights of potentiality capable for our own embodiment.

To authentically acknowledge your own living capability of becoming an enlightened version of yourself, you must first acknowledge that there are actually beings who have already become united with the absolute highest version of their sense of self.

We all stand on the shoulders of spiritual giants, those who climbed until they reached their ultimate potential. By studying and honoring those beings who have carried the torch of enlightenment before us, an unshakable belief in human consciousness and the spiritual capabilities that are hiding therein begin to fully dawn.

Every guru and yogi and buddha and divine mother and avatar are all consciously united with the higher self of us all. In this sense, they are each literally your very own higher self.

The more fully you recognize the enlightened incarnations of humanity's history as being inextricably intertwined with your own being, the more you are propelled on the path towards becoming your own version of the one enlightened self which manifests through many faces.

Behind all veils of illusion, the intelligence of the infinite is a singular witness that shines through all of life and the presence of all awakened beings.

The eternal teacher is the oneness of radiant knowingness, the one light of truth which has appeared in the refracted forms of all the masters over the course of phenomena's history.

If you truly attain your enlightened potential, you are actually becoming one with the same eternally enlightened cosmic mind which has been actualized and incarnated through every other enlightened being ever to be.

God is in all things, is the source of all things, remains transcendent of all things, yet also exists like a seed in us all waiting to blossom into an enlightened self-expression. The dormant enlightened energy in each of us is the kundalini shakti which grows like a tree through the physical, subtle, and astral bodies until the causal body is fully present in each of the lower sheaths of self.

Each guru is like a fully grown, fruit-producing tree. Each tree has the power to spread numerous seeds, or activate the kundalini shakti in and number of authentically seeking spiritual aspirants.

In the presence of a true guru, you have all you need to attain a glimpse of the state of enlightenment. In fact, a fundamental aspect of any being in an enlightened state is that they can instantaneously awaken any other being who is open enough through a transmission of intention, gaze, touch, or word. Being in the presence of a true guru is technically all you need to attain enlightenment.

True gurus are often humble, simple, and detached from material wealth. That doesn't mean that all gurus should never live lavishly, just that they should have no need to hyper-fixate attachment on material abundance or worldly recognition.

The historical example most often cited in regards to the proper attitude for a guru to hold towards wealth and comfort is that of Sage Vasistha.

Vasistha was the guru of ancient kings throughout history. Whenever they called upon his guidance, a parade of messengers brought Vasistha to the kings with grandiose royal splendor. Vasistha would be brought out of his hut of solitude in the middle of the woods where he wore bark as clothes and ate only what he foraged, into the pomp and circumstance of royal living. There he would be fed delicacies, dressed in fine clothing, and treated with the utmost respect. When his counsel was no longer needed or the call for movement arose clearly within him, he was brought back to his simple place of dwelling and continued on with his austere way of life without any sense of duality between these environments.

Many people often wondered why he didn't stay with royal families and live lavishly all the time, but Vasistha had absolutely no attachment to one lifestyle or the other.

When he lived with kings, Vasistha lived like a king. When he lived in the woods, Vasistha lived in stoic simplicity.

He didn't attach to the abundance and he didn't cling to the austerity as some merit badge of self-righteous spirituality.

This is the way of a true guru.

The only thing a true guru is fixated upon is union with the indwelling, radiant intelligence of the Divine.

They are so attuned to the infinite that miracles and spontaneous blessings pour out of them without effort. In the presence of the true spiritual master, people automatically go into deep meditation, experience phenomenal vision, and open to extra dimensional occurrences.

This is all according to the desire of the disciple and not the will of the guru.

The real masters do not intentionally manipulate their students in any way. The guru simply puts total faith in the transformational power of the Divine and allows it to guide each student accordingly.

They emanate, sit back and witness.

If you seek enlightenment, you will automatically reach attainment through serving the guru. If you seek material prosperity, to bear a child, achieve fame, or any particular blessing within form then that is what you will receive from the grace of the guru's shakti.

If you go into trance, it is the Divine energy establishing itself in your mind-sphere and not the guru pulling on you like some mischievous puppet master who tricks and mesmerizes.

True trance, which is known as bhava samadhi, and the guru's grace manifesting in any form through the body, which are known as kriyas, are a far cry from hypnotism. Hypnotists and gurus are beings with completely opposite approaches. One tries to manipulate you while the other teaches you how to be free from human suffering and delusive self-manipulation which all unenlightened egos engage.

A true guru is so unshakably united with the energy of the infinite that they can automatically transmit this awakened state to anyone who enters their presence. They are like fountains overflowing with the nectar of bliss, all you have to do is fill a cup up and drink. This transmission of awakened energy is known as darshan. Darshan is the blessing of being in the presence of an enlightened being.

When you bow to a guru you are drinking the divine nectar which overflows from the vessel of their form, you are becoming receptive in a way that allows their subtle energy field to penetrate your own. The subtle energy is known to come down through the crown of the awakened-form's head and pass through their bodies, exiting from the fingertips and feet.

This is why you often see gurus bestowing blessings through hand gesture or see students touching their feet. By bowing to a guru you are acknowledging that they have become one with God, so you are also simultaneously acknowledging your own potential of also becoming one with God.

Touching the feet of a guru is not about lowering yourself, it is a technology of subtle energy transmission. Bowing is not about duality in any way, it should not be viewed as a degrading activity. In fact, there is nothing more empowering than bowing to a true guru because it fills you with the utmost essence of your potential.

Other traditional methods of gurus transmitting shakti include blessing food known as prasad or infusing shakti in elemental sources such as a flame or bowl of water. Even just thinking of the guru brings their literal presence into your awareness-stream. You can visualize them blessing you and your meals and activities or call upon them by simply looking at their picture. Their blessings will come into your life.

The next level of deepening the connection to the guru is known as shaktipat. Shaktipat is when the guru establishes an unbreakable energy bond beyond your being and theirs in such a way that a complete transfer of their enlightened state occurs over the course of your incarnation.

This is different then darshan in the sense that when the energy of darshan passes through you it then dissipates over the course of a day or two if you do not utilize it to the highest degree. The blessings of many darshans over a lifetime will undoubtedly transform you, but receiving shaktipat means the energy of the master is constantly being replenished in your being through an unbroken stream of blessings.

Shaktipat is a commitment by the guru to bring the student to enlightenment, but it is also a commitment on the part of the student to live in such a way that regulates their awareness through spiritual discipline. As the shakti fully enters your being, it awakens the storehouse of subliminal kundalini shakti living in the base of your spine and works its way up the subtle energy path near spinal column, called the sushumna, until it pierces your crown and leads you to complete God-Realization.

The techniques which lead to the attainment of enlightenment can essentially be qualified as yoga. To become a true yogi you must complete what is known as tapas. Tapas is a regime of extreme spiritual discipline that is carried out from the point of self-realization all the way to the point of God-Realization. Only those who have completed tapas can rightfully be considered yogis.

Just because you practice yoga does not mean you are a yogi.

Other enlightened masters have achieved unshakable attainment in previous births and do not need to go through the entire process of tapas to attain enlightenment in this life.

They are known as avatars.

The use of the word avatar means someone who is enlightened at birth and maintains that completed state of wakefulness throughout their entire incarnation.

Whether they are an avatar or a yogi, a true guru is marked by their ability to transmit shakti. You will be able to tell the fully realized master from the partially realized spiritual teacher if you really look closely enough.

The role of the guru is specifically to initiate and guide other beings into an enlightened state. This may be on a public scale or a private one, but the function is the same.

The master pulses with Divine energy to such a degree that they are often swaying in harmony with an invisible breeze of subtle energy.

The master is a lion bursting with raw wakefulness and yet can often appear gentle as a kitten. Devotion to these beings and the Divine intelligence they embody is rocket fuel which directly converts to spiritual progress. Attaining an awakened state requires momentum and the guru provides the boost needed to get this ball rolling way to the infinite degree.

All gurus live in each guru.

In this sense, your future-higher self lives through their current selves. The chain of enlightened beings in an unbroken connection of torchbearers.

This human birth is an extremely precious opportunity to actualize your mystic potential. It is very rare to incarnate with a human birth and unlike any other species it allows us to work on our karma by striving towards enlightenment. This is a golden opportunity for your awakening and the fact that you are reading these words means you have an inherent inclination towards fulfilling this grandest arc of evolution.

You never know when death will come knocking on your door, you may never have a chance to wholeheartedly pursue your enlightenment if you do not seize this very moment as your sign to begin to practicing daily spiritual disciplines such as meditation.

To avoid this rare timing is like throwing away a winning lottery ticket. Karma is very subtle. No effort, big or small, is ever lost in the chain of cause and effect. Anything you can do to fulfill the potential of this human birth will bless you in exponential measure.

Every moment is a fleeting expression of the Divine and it would be a sad loss to waste the opportunity of this birth.

In this very moment, there is nothing more valuable than taking refuge in the lifestyle of spiritual discipline and following the path set forth by the spiritual masters.

The guru has externally manifest to show us the way to God, but the guru also lives within each of us as our own inner clarity, intuition, and intelligence. This intelligence must be fostered in its ultimate form by practicing meditation, and complimentary disciplines, every single day.

This is the only way you will ever come to know your higher self, your higher potential, and your true connection to the source of all creation.

If you come to know your mind in the truest sense you will be the Buddha.

To fully be the Buddha and to live fully as your Buddha-self, it will be supremely helpful to study the many forms of those who have already attained total enlightenment

There is no other external path that is more helpful for your path towards awakening yourself and humanity than working with a guru.

The guru is the ultimate expression of humanity and evolution. A true guru is one with the consciousness that pervades all of creation, one with the singular soul which resides in all beings, and therefore the guru is your very own nature in its highest expression.

The guru is your higher self, your true potential, and your ultimate destiny.

To receive the shakti of a true guru is like being given a glimpse of your own future. They allow you to glimpse what you will grow into and allow you to attain unshakable faith in greater process of eternity.

This will encourage you to strive in increasingly larger leaps and bounds towards your own Divine potential. They will show you the value of the process of living within the realms of spiritual self effort by their lives reflecting a completed example of existence's ultimate fruition.

In honoring the guru, you will soon bloom into your own higher self. Without seeing a tree, you cannot know what a tree is.

Read all the books you want, but when you see a truly realized master you will know your own capability and be inspired to grow and grow and grow until you too can provide shade and nourishment for those needing shelter on the path.

This is the greatest service to humanity and the strongest force which will ultimately be what transforms society from within.

20: SADHANA UNIT THEORY

The degree to which you witness the true nature of phenomenon as embodied by your guru will be correspondingly infused into your Divine aspiration of spiritual attainment. By observing a fully actualized guru, the latent potential of inhabiting your divinity begins to swell. A tidal wave of enthusiasm will come over your being once you realize the true profundity that is hiding in plain sight. Bodhichitta is the principle which represents a mind set on awakening. The mind set on awakening is the mindset of awakening. There is no asset more valuable on the journey of spiritual awakening than bodhichitta. The more you dial into your latent spiritual potential and embrace the lifestyle required to actualize this potential, the faster you will evolve towards the infinite.

You must build a lifestyle geared towards awakening that is authentic to you according to your energy levels, your mental disposition, your cultural and religious leanings, your capacity for practice, and your chosen form of the Divine or the guru. However this formula of wakefulness looks according to you, it will inevitably incorporate daily spiritual discipline or sadhana (sadha-na). Sadhana is any practice that you do every day (regardless of how much your mind resists or your scheduling preferences differ) to maintain your attunement to formlessness.

At first, your daily disciplines may only constitute a few moments or minutes of meditation and other spiritual practices, but according to your degree of bodhichitta it can naturally grow with great ease.

Until you put your spiritual awakening into the active context of doing practices, it will remain a mental construct and therefore, impart an ego-complex. The level of intensity of your practice will in turn inform the degree of enlightenment you come to possess. Your connection to the illumined mind-sphere is in direct correlation to your sadhana, more so than any vision you've had or epiphany you have reached. It is always determined by your current state of presence and the current state of your practice of attunement to the living qualities of empty-luminosity. You are never more enlightened then what your most recent meditation reflects.

Your practice, although a discipline, doesn't have to feel like a chore. The process of emerging into your awakened identity can be fully joyful when approached properly.

In fact, the more you can engineer your approach so that your practice doesn't feel like a chore, the more rapid and fruitful your sadhana will be. The spontaneity and blissfulness of the beyond are essential ingredients to the cosmic soup of form which can't be ignored in your approach to the practice of masterful embodiment.

Through recognizing the world as a true illusion, the natural approach to your sadhana should be treating it like a game. Make sure to have some fun as you level up. The gamification of your practices is an unbelievably underrated god-head hack.

Don't take enlightenment too seriously or it won't take you too seriously either.

When you cry for God, God quietly comforts you. When you joyously laugh at the passing show of phenomena, God is also laughing with you and as you.

Embracing your sadhana with joy and humor creates positive reinforcement within your conditioned neurological response to the process itself. Rewiring these pathways of response to spiritual discipline actually makes you crave the process and flow right into your enlightened potential. Dopamine is released in our brains when we laugh and when we play. True spiritual masters are often simultaneously the most serious and relaxed people you will ever meet.

Another way to release dopamine in your brain is through experiencing the feeling of being "on the right track". By treating your journey to enlightenment like a game, your brain creates a positive feedback loop with each session of daily disciplines that you complete, as well as at each stage of inner insight you achieve through your sadhana.

If you treat yourself like a hero on a hero's journey, your brain will reward you accordingly. In general, life will reward you by giving you clues, signposts, and guides if you seek, look, and embark upon the ultimate journey to the soul.

It is easy to be daunted by the vastness of the journey. This is a journey that requires tremendous self-effort. The simple truth of the path up the mountain is that it is always completed one step at a time.

Sometimes you will leap, perhaps at other times you will crawl.

Whatever happens, just keep moving.

It is helpful to break your quest for enlightenment down into digestible fragments.

Treat each session of your sadhana as a singular unit of energy, activity, or consciousness. Do not judge each session by the hours or seconds comprising its constitution.

Each unit is like a building block in the construction of your Divine life, a single grain of sand in your mandala palace. Your units may start as mere minutes or moments, but soon your units will add up to much more. After a few days your units can add up to hours, and before you know it become entire days, weeks, months, years, and lifetimes of fulfilling self-effort if your bodhichitta allows.

The surest way is to let the energy of your sadhana units grow steadily and slowly.

Don't get down on yourself if you are currently only able to meditate for five or ten minutes at a time. Revel in those minutes. Try to make them the most nourishing and inner thirst-quenching few minutes you can possibly imagine.

As you begin to expand into the joy held within each unit, the units will slowly expand in duration and you will equally expand in your capacity for larger and more frequent units comprised of more vast and blissful experiences.

The consistency and regularity of doing daily sadhana units is invaluable. If you never stray too far from your practice, neither will the Divine.

An equally valuable approach to your practice is to break down your daily units into digestible portions throughout the day. By doing two to four sessions a day, you never venture too far into the illusion and can quickly come back to God's presence as the baseline recognition orchestrating your experience reality. Soon doing sadhana will become your source of refreshment and your practice will become a safe haven that inspires pure joy and consists of no struggle.

Allow yourself to be fluid and adaptable with your units as you grow into your evolving capacity for spiritual discipline.

Leave a gap between you and your attachment to the rigidness of your approach because spirit is infinite, and therefore your capacity for meditation is liable to make unexpected jumps of exponential proportions.

Over the course of months and years, your ability to expand your sadhana units will astound you.

There will be thresholds you break that never seemed possible, but the growth will likely come in waves.

As you reach the capacity of practicing for several hours a day, you may not be able to immediately stabilize in this lifestyle for the rest of your life and this should not be viewed as a problem. Sometimes the tides are high, sometimes low.

When you reach that point it will be worth considering an approach of taking on periodical stretches of total retreat into meditative seclusion, anustahn, or "installation of the ultimate". To grow into your meditative potential properly you must give your body, emotions, mind, and lifestyle room for adjustment, time for refractory periods before as well as after these growth spurts of actualization and meditative seclusion.

True tapas is not something that can be forced. However, the more you find comfort within this approach of sadhana unit theory, the more you will be able to grow your energy modules in such a way that moves you in swift strides towards an eventual tapas and establishment of total enlightenment.

You can't manipulate God into granting you enlightenment, yet it is your self-effort that directly causes the grace to allow your spiritual growth and that capacity is something you have to negotiate within yourself.

If you can meditate for the stretch of an hour at a time, you will soon be able to meditate for two or more sessions of one hour stretches at a time in a day.

If you can handle units of sadhana to such a degree, you will soon be able to do back to back units of an hour or so, two to four times a day.

Before you know it, the one-hour meditation unit of sadhana will easily lead you to the capacity for sitting in meditation for four to eight hours per day, casually.

This approach to sadden unit theory is how you really strengthen and build your yogic muscles to train for tapas without strain.

Naturally, there will be waves of bodhichitta-filled enthusiasm and lulls with lesser degrees of it.

As you build up to doing anustahns and meditative retreats of the like once every year or so, you may find yourself drifting back down to less sadhana a day in between those peaks of self-effort.

This is not a bad thing. You are preparing yourself to relate to the infinite nature of consciousness and this takes some major adjusting to master.

At the beginning of practicing anustahns and unit expansions, these energies will purge your physical, emotional, and mental karmas. Slowly, as you continue to deepen your awareness of the inner light, you will begin to bask in heightened joyousness, profound contentedness, vibrant playfulness, and a spontaneous desire to spread this newfound Divine love to everyone you encounter.

You will begin to see others walking under the spell of ego-identification and separatism as if they are living in a dream state. You will no longer even recognize or remember feeling many of the lower human attachments and delusions which once bound you by hand and foot. Your stifling habits will naturally be purified and leave you free of the gripping intensities which plague so much of humanity.

It may not happen all at once, at first you may even experience waves of heightened human desire and heightened grasping for external gratification as the subtle energy begins to surge through your being. If you continue to practice through the waves of clinging, slowly all your unwanted difficulties will shed of their own accord.

Eventually, through your spiritual disciplines, you will find yourself effortlessly resting in the naturally calm center of your being.

You will gently witness all of life as a passing show.

It is such a glorious feeling to arrive fully in the here and now.

There is a Divine bath of inner bliss awaiting you as you return to your natural enlightenment.

You may, at a certain point in your sadhana, feel there is no need to continue with your spiritual disciplines.

Never forget the entangling nature of illusion, each day new delusions will fascinate you. Therefore, even following your total realization of the Divine, you must continue to practice some forms of purifying disciplines as we are all inherently unified with the soul level.

The greatest spiritual masters continually practice relating to the inner expanse of peace every day despite fully identifying as enlightened.

There is no end to the expansion into infinity.

Your insight will always continue to blossom.

Your compassion will always continue to flourish.

You must simply continue doing the practices with detachment and persistence. It will be must easier to maintain this high level of spiritual practice if you don't think about it too much.

Just do the practices without always second-guessing how much they are benefiting your moment to moment existence or how close you are getting to enlightenment. God's nature is infinite and the growth through sadhana is also unending, even for those who have already attained enlightenment.

All will be forthcoming through continuing to engage your sadhana units each day.

You will consciously expand into the space beyond the beyond.

You will attune to the most subtle aspects of energy and become one with the essence of energy itself.

In becoming one with the Divine in your identification and through daily sadhana, you will become completely empowered to the point of living as an unshakeable bridge between the subtle and physical worlds.

Through your sadhana, you will become the very force of heaven which will transform the Earth.

PART FOUR:

ETERNAL REALMS

21: COSMIC LAW

There has been a fascinating discovery in the sonic sector of scientific study called cymatics. If you take a flat surface covered with sand or another granular object, and introduce a slowly increasing tonal frequency directly below that plane – you will witness something quite remarkable. As the frequency of the tone increases, patterns naturally begin to emerge in the sand. Initially, these geometric patterns are rather simple, but the patterns become increasingly more intricate in design as the frequency increases. Some sonic regions throughout the spectrum of frequencies are more precisely geometric or symmetrical than others and tend to lock into plateaus of patterns, but the trend of increased intricacy continues throughout.

Another fascinating aspect of this sonic experiment is that in between each of the patterns, there is a recurring lull of cyclical chaos where the granular object scatters in a seemingly random fashion before reestablishing its newly heightened expression of form. If you haven't seen this before or heard of cymatics, it is definitely worth looking up a video of this unique reflection.

Cymatics are more than just an experiment with sound and sand, they are a metaphor. Increasing the frequency of a sound effects matter correlatively. This is true on physical and subtle levels.

Just as the vibration of energy comprising our collective species' consciousness increases over the arc of evolution, the same journey through form can be observed in cymatics. In one case it is occurring on the macrocosmic level of the procession of the patterns constituting the intelligence of the universe, while in the other (cymatics), it is expressed through the microcosm of sand. The movement through frequencies manifests on a cosmic scale expresses the same progression on a dimensional scale relative to what is microcosmically expressed through the sand in experiments with cymatics.

Each of the formations of geometry can be related to the invisible laws of dimensionality which comprise the nature of each realm within creation.

The ultimate macrocosm of chaotic expression which alternates between the cycles of form, and facilities the transitions between dimensions, can be related to the notions of the bardo or the void.

Only through the unknown can we reach new heights of order and consciousness.

In wholeheartedly knowing the connection between vibration and consciousness, the same metaphor of the patterns in cymatics can be applied to our figurative understanding of the literal developmental shifts happening in the different periods of human civilization and greater epochs of cosmological processions.

Society moves through a progression of intricacies in perfect unison with the evolution of the consciousness held by its citizens.

This also means that society naturally must undergo refractory periods of chaos between each new period of advancement in each of the relative spheres in each of the singularities comprising the triad.

This alternating pattern of order and chaos is a natural sequence of cycles which occurs on all levels of reality, including the construction of human civilization. The discomfort and difficulty from the chaos in our society is preparing us for an era of greater unity.

As we collectively move towards establishing an enlightened society, moving through increased periods of disarray is unavoidable.

The rules of law governing subtle energy are microcosmically represented through so many reflections on different scales throughout the myriad of all phenomena, such as in the study of cymatics.

This metaphor has many, many levels of implication.

For one, it is completely natural that we are experiencing the degradation of society. It is not ideal in the sense that so many are suffering, but it is ideal in the sense that these are signs of progression within the evolving human project of humanity.

Another reflection held within the metaphor of cymatics is that the most intricately subtle laws of nature are hiding in plain sight and often have yet to be discovered. Eventually, the inner workings of the hidden laws of nature will reveal themselves as we continue to evolve into higher expressions of embodying consciousness.

The sophistication of order required to regulate an enlightened society will arise in due time. As long as we continue to increase the frequency of our consciousnesses through spiritual discipline, even when we witness cyclical periods of chaotic formations of energy sequences all will be forthcoming.

If, in the recognition of ensuing chaos, we collectively descend into animalistic reactiveness then the resultant patterns of society will not properly evolve into its next iteration of sequences required for society's eventual enlightenment.

Our perception, state of awareness, and corresponding relationship to consciousness fundamentally alter the mechanics of reality as we know it. Quantum physics is a great reflection of this phenomenon.

We may not yet fully understand all the rules of quantum mechanics, but we do know that particles are in an ambiguous state until perceived.

Once particles are witnessed they go from being in the seemingly paradoxical state of potentially inhabiting multiple positions simultaneously, to being locked into a fixed state and location.

Quantum positioning implies that, on some fundamental level, energy is effected by being perceived and responds to this influence.

The implications of quantum positioning, and other aspects of quantum mechanics, are unfathomably vast.

The human mind does not yet fully understand all the implications of quantum physics, but the fact that particles respond to being perceived clearly implies the interconnectivity of awareness and matter on a particular level.

How do particles instantly respond to being perceived by fixing their position?

The exact formulaic expressions of the science underlying this phenomenon are unclear at this time, but it undeniably implies that there are innate levels of intelligence and self-awareness on an energetic level.

When we perceive phenomena, it shifts to match our perception of it.

There is a difference between perception and reality.

Most people conceptually understand that things are not always as they appear. It is easy to recognize this truth on the level that our interpretation of events does not always match the reality of the events that have unfolded; however, most have yet to contemplate how this notion applies to how humanity's collective degree of self-awareness effects the literal laws which reality operates according to.

The subtle laws of nature which apply to our experience of reality shift as our consciousnesses evolve.

Our faith in the latent potentiality of how reality can unfold fundamentally effects the way that reality actually does unfold.

The more we know about the innate laws of energy through studying the subtle qualities of our own perceptions, the more the literal laws of physics will express themselves in a correspondingly subtle manner of sophistication.

In the yogic traditions, reality is known to assume the basic nature of Satchitananda (Sat-Chit-Ananda).

This means that the fundamental qualities of the essence of energy are Sat (existence), Chit (intelligence), and Ananda (bliss).

As we evolve into higher states of awareness, reality actively expresses the more exquisite aspects of its nature as beingness, knowingness, and blissfulness.

As we come to understand the subtle laws which are intrinsic to reality, we will slowly move through the inter dimensional hierarchy of the laws of form (just like the patterns of sand does in cymatics).

The movement from collectively identifying with reality as material-derived to consciousness-based will lead us through the spectrum of dimensions until we fully manifest the highest of realms.

It is actually through the merit of spiritual austerities being performed by cosmic entities that the material realms are formed in the first place.

It is also through spiritual disciplines that the material realms are fundamentally maintained by the Divine.

It is therefore through spiritual disciplines that the material realms will be transmuted back into Divine realms to the point where we will literally come to remember ourselves as the eternal and cosmic entities that started this whole journey through the patterns of life-forms.

The wheel of karma is turned by the energetic aftermath of the ceremonies conducted in the realms of angels, gods, and buddhas.

As we perform spiritual practices ourselves, we become one with those very angels, gods, and buddhas which in turn elevates our dimension of collective, human operation until our reality and the Divine are fully united in function.

The lower expressions of realms are kept in position by our suffering and confusion. Negative emotion is the glue that binds the illusion together and the nectar that satisfies the glutinous demons feeding off our reality.

As you transition from fixating upon suffering to transforming it through spiritual practices, you ascend into higher realms.

As we come into collectively normalizing the culture of spiritual discipline, the entirety of society ascends into the higher realms.

This principle is not a mere abstraction. Our consciousnesses fundamentally alter the ways in which life is manifesting.

Our culturally maintained, materialist's view of our fundamental separateness and sense of identifying with duality keeps us locked in a lower form of reality.

Human society not only maintain a materialist view of reality, but has constructed an entire system of self-governance which corresponds to placing our value in the production and quantifiable attachment to material goods and culture.

To establish an enlightened society, we will soon have to evolve past the point of inferring that the value of human life is based on economic worth. Equally so, we will have to evolve past our view of the world as a material realm all together if we wish to move into understanding the subtle laws which govern the formulation of phenomenon.

Beyond any other quality, energy is fundamentally an expression of emptiness. Understanding the simultaneous possibility of emptiness and Divine intelligence comprising the essence of energy is a major key in unlocking the secrets of the subtler laws of physics.

Similarly, creating a system of global governance without the ego-driven self-interest of elitists as the primary quality controlling our lives is a major key in transcending this era where those in power are massively oppressing the majority of our population.

This approach has consistently lead us back down into the chaotic cycles of revolutions which are currently required to acquire basic human justice. Both the individual and societal journeys of evolution are expedited by each of us taking on the disciplines of daily meditation and other practices of spiritual self-effort.

We must create a system that encourages self-discovery while simultaneously rewarding those who serve the needs of the system at large. This must be done without withholding anyone's basic human needs as blackmail in the process.

To ensure the moral uprightness of those who attempt to orchestrate and govern a system that benefits humanity, as an enlightened society will necessitate, we all must participate in spiritual self-effort or else we are doomed to fail in the due course of the corruptibility of the mind. Mind control is the key to functioning as an enlightened society.

There is an allegory that is commonly told about a council of owls. Since the owls are only awake at night, none of them have ever seen the sun. The wisest of owls determined and conveyed to the council that since none of them have ever seen the sun, that there in fact is no sun. They have heard of it, but none of them have personally experienced or witnessed the sun's existence due to their nocturnal nature.

Similarly, since we have never truly had enlightened leadership on a global level in the modern era, most do not believe that an enlightened society is even possible.

Since we have never seen a globally harmonious system of governance, we don't really believe it is actually achievable. Equally so, since most have never seen God, society has become increasingly atheistic.

All of these roadblocks on the path to the golden era will be overcome with the same master key: a culture which fully integrates the practice of daily meditation.

22: DIMENSIONAL SHIFT

Every situation is more than a situation.

Every situation is a reflection of the psychological disposition of each being who participates in it's construction.

Every realm can primarily be defined by the collective level of consciousness maintained by the individuals inhabiting it.

The same geographic location can foster any level of consciousness within the spectrum of realms. Each individual is inhabiting a realm according to their specific psychology while the community of individuals inhabiting an environment also creates a collective realm according to the psychological state that they mutually inhabit.

A term used in Yogic traditions that has become commonly misunderstood throughout modern spiritual communities is 'mandala'.

On one level, a mandala is a geometric configuration which usually contains varying degrees of symmetry.

On another level, a mandala correlates to the realms of psychology within any given tier of the potential circumstances possible in the experience of phenomena.

Both levels of the mandala principle are subtly interconnected and are both invisibly functioning features of every dimension throughout space-time and beyond.

These two levels of subtle circuitry are at play in every circumstance whether one is aware of it or not.

The mandala principle is the determining factor that defines which dimension, or series of planes, an individual is operating in.

The word dimension can be used to denote aspects of reality such as space or time. It can be used to denote the qualities of a circumstance such as emotion or color palate. However, in this case the word dimension is used interchangeably with the words realm and sphere to denote the different planes of consciousness such as human, animal, hungry ghost, god, or buddha. Each of these mandala realms have their own corresponding geometry and psychology.

The connection between vibration, sound, and form also implies that each dimension has its own corresponding sound structure (which is another way to say mantra) that microcosmically reflects the entire realm. Another subtle facet implicated is that each realm has a governing entity correlated to its vibrational composition who corresponds through form to the consciousness of the entire realm.

The dimension you inhabit (with its corresponding mandala of geometry, psychology, mantra, and presiding deity) is all dependent on the level of consciousness you maintain and therefore how you direct your attention.

Each mandala-realm (or plane of consciousness) exists in the bubble of its own independent function, but simultaneously synchronizes with the whole web of interconnected mandala-spheres which comprise the entirety of all phenomena in creation.

This web of spheres of existing mandalas exists in a vaster mandala of webbed spheres of mandala realms which is a mandala unto itself.

This multi-tiered fractal of the mandala principle is akin to how we each simultaneously exist physically in a town, a nation, a continent, a planet, a solar system, a galaxy, and a universe without those locations being mutually exclusive or interfering with one another's role in your place of being.

The same is true dimensionally in all space and psychologically in relation to the subtle realms.

You exist in the realm of your own mentality, a shared realm with those who have similar mentalities on this planet, a shared realm of self-similar collective psychology in the spectrum of all collective psychological spheres throughout all the parallel universes in existence, and the shared realm where that collective of parallel universes fits into the spectrum of dimensions throughout all of the planes of consciousness. None of these are mutually exclusive realms or dimensions, we each inhabit them all simultaneously. They all are concurrently in operation for each of us relative to our state of consciousness, although most entities are hardly aware of the first tier of these spheres.

This notion of spheres of mandala-realms can also be visualized in a more microcosmic manner. In this way, the mandala principle is akin to chemistry.

A web of particles interconnects to make an element just as a collection of psychologies interconnect to comprise an individual's mandala-realm. Each person's collection of different modes of emotion, thought, and action makes up their immediate mandala-sphere.

In so many senses, all of these complicated notions regarding spheres of realms comes down to the simple principle of directing awareness.

Your attention corresponds to your level of awareness and therefore corresponds to the degree of dimensionality comprising the level of reality in which you reside.

You are what you eat or in this case, your realm follows your attention.

A buddha is still a buddha whether walking through heaven or earth.

When you exist beyond the dualities of the lower mind, there is no need to assess which plane you are on. Simply focus on blissful immersion with limitless spirit.

The psychological wakefulness we each possess determines who is a buddha; not where we live, with whom we associate, or how we look.

The physical attributes of a plane will always be secondary to the psychological attributes of those who inhabit any given realm in determining which dimension is truly being inhabited.

Jesus was able to exist on Earth, which is supposedly a human realm. His ability to walk on water and awaken the dead defies the properties of human realms as most have come to know them.

The psychology of Jesus was far more exquisite than the psychology of the average human and, in that sense, Jesus didn't live in the human realm at all.

To transform the human realm of Earth into a higher dimension, we have to transform our psychologies in such a way that gives room for the laws of physics on our plane to transform into the subtle laws of higher realms. It is only through spiritual self-effort that we will come to have enough faith to properly experience the magic of life. In doing so we will transform ourselves as to more fully witness and live in alignment with the Divine.

The laws of nature and the rules of physics are bound by the specific mandala-realm being inhabited. As humanity collectively elevates its awareness, we will all elevate our inhabited mandala-sphere.

To truly create a heaven out of the Earth, we each must refine our awarenesses. Through our individual evolution from being materially identified to becoming identified with spirit, we can each reach a level of potential that most humans have only heard about in fairy tales and scriptures.

Many have read about Jesus turning water into wine, healing the diseased, and resurrecting after the crucifixion, but how many have truly contemplated the state of consciousness required to operate in such a way that is so very alive with infinite potentiality?

This is the requirement to make a heaven of Earth.

We are talking about undermining gravity and defying death.

We are talking about the manipulation of subatomic particles in such a way that flight and other yogic powers (known as siddhis) become a normalized part of our existences.

This advancement of inner capability will fundamentally transform the need and impulse towards our advancements in outer technology, cultural acclaim, and political influence over time.

A dozen or so beings capable of completely transforming the appearance of our shared reality using their wills alone could instantaneously save Earth from all impending environmental calamities and stop any nuclear bomb in its tracks.

Many scriptures have declared that a few enlightened masters living in caves are already actively preventing our planet from descending into total catastrophe through their spiritually attained psychic abilities.

Imagine if humanity were brimming with such beings.

In such a world, there would be no need for phones since if we could communicate telepathically nor airplanes if we could fly yogically (or perhaps even teleport inter dimensionally at will).

Most have heard of the technological capabilities of aliens and the spiritually healing capabilities of angels, but how many truly believe that humanity could ever reach such states of function?

These sorts of capabilities are not only limited by our collective consciousness, but also the degree of moral uprightness maintained by our species.

Beings with such powers could quickly destroy the planet if they were operating out of egotism. Fortunately for us all, to achieve such heights of yogic power the individual must be completely attuned to the subtle. To be attuned to the subtle, we must live and breathe in harmony with all things to such a degree that some sense of fundamental compassion must inherently have been achieved.

In the scriptures of nearly every major religion it is taught that the prophets always return to Earth when humanity is in its darkest state and is in greatest need for spiritual resuscitation. The incarnation of enlightened masters always corresponds to the needs of each era, and it really is starting to seem like this era is in need. How each prophet presents themselves is in accordance to the needs of the people and relative to the state of the collective consciousness held in each era.

The state of humanity's collective consciousness in each era goes through natural cycles of ascending and descending orders. Currently, however one linearly qualifies our eras of collective consciousness, humanity is undergoing a highly tension-filled time.

Now is our time to strive, this moment is our chance to aspire, this very incarnation is your best shot to become fully united with your inherent divinity.

It is humanity's destiny to bring heaven to Earth, Zion into Babylon, Eden back to Africa.

This transformation will not only require expanding our consciousness, but also will require the expansion of our compassion. This transition will demand that each of us to master ourselves and therefore become the masters of our own mandala-spheres.

We each must learn to live as the rulers of our own universes, as the lords of our own realms. God is the king of us all, but we must each learn to live like the rulers of our own realms, the masters of our own mind-mandalas, the kings and queens of our own heavens.

We are each responsible for the evolutionary shifts of the collective dimensions by intentionally shifting our own dimensions.

The responsibility for our collective fate is in the hands of each of us. No one can do it for you, although a true guru can grant you a glimpse.

No one can believe for you, although a true guru can show you a living example of total faith.

No one can take us there, although a true guru is already living in their own heaven and in meeting them we jump through a portal into a higher dimension and see the mirror of our own minds reflecting a higher dimension of our own self.

We have to begin by acting as if we have the potential for enlightenment if we wish to achieve enlightenment.

We must each come to know that every pore of our skin literally holds millions of universes in accordance with the fractalization of interconnected mandala-spheres comprising reality.

Infinite dimensions are hiding in plain sight.

Nothing is disconnected and everything is interwoven in ways that will continue to blow our rational minds moment after moment when we truly begin to see reality as it is.

Seeing everything as non-dual, which is known as vedanta, will allow us to understand the path from here to heaven.

The gateway to shifting our dimension of operation is held in the elevation and refinement of our perceptions of reality.

The shift evolves through each individual, one being at a time. However, the collective transition from Earth to some form of heaven will require a culture-wide shift towards inner attunement if we wish to actually achieve the heights of our dormant, Divine potential as a species.

23: THE ALTAR OF NOW

It is of unquestionably urgent importance to address the conflicts that are arising throughout the world. Simultaneously, we must not lose sight of the fact that there are natural phases of collective evolution and each is filled with different degrees of necessary growing pains.

There is a saying from the mystic tradition of Judaism which states that there are only two forces operating in all of Creation: blessings and hidden blessings. The immediate implication can be found in context of the fact that everything is functioning according to the co-dependent nature of their arising and undeniable interconnectedness of their occurrence. All of form is in a grand synchronization and therefore has some meaningfulness or purpose in its orientation in space-time. Also, the fact that anything is occurring at all is quite miraculous.

The notion of perceiving existence as being a combination of blessings and hidden blessings is not an excuse for spiritually bypassing the problems at hand.

To truly establish heaven on Earth we must tirelessly work towards bettering our embodiments of harmony.

We won't be able to collectively live in the fullness of humanity's compassionate potential until the highest view of interconnectedness and non-duality dawns in each of our individual senses of identification.

To glimpse what our lives would functionally consist of in a timeless realm, we must each cultivate our own iteration of self-mastery relative to our individual life paths.

Through our own sublime actualization, we each bring these ideals forth into our habits, lives, and the world at large. Eventually, enough beings will wholeheartedly fulfill the project of bringing themselves into a heavenly state that it will overflow abundantly and reform society.

For society to be considered truly civilized requires everyone's needs for a life in which their basic dignity to be authentically met. Earth cannot become Heaven without making it possible for everyone to have food, water, shelter, education, healthcare, and the opportunity to meaningfully contribute to the greater human project in a unique way.

We all know what it is like to suffer. The Buddha taught that this is unavoidable in the human experience. Since we all know the grave intensity of experiencing human suffering, why wouldn't those in power work more authentically to ensure that no one on Earth has to experience any greater difficulty than is absolutely necessary in this life? The short answer is: the ego.

We can't develop a system that satisfies everyone's basic human needs until we learn to satisfy our innermost yearning for transcending the ego.

We can't create a system that satisfies the needs of the people as long as we don't fully understand our interconnectedness.

Only once we pursue the heaven that is living in our hearts will we be able to conceive of a world that functions with an intricate and heavenly design.

To mitigate all the problems of our world, we must first mitigate all the problems created by the ignorances egoically plaguing our minds.

The attitude of non-duality will open the door to our collective heavenly abode.

While meditation is the master key, living with the view of non-duality is the act of opening of the door.

When you view all as your very own Self, you feel an unquestionable urge to serve all beings as your very own Self.

We are all truly one being looking through many eyes.

If we wish to cultivate Heaven on Earth, we must look into every pair of eyes and learn to see only Self.

This doesn't mean that we all have to live the same way or even believe all the same things, but what it does mean is that we have to work together.

We must infuse compassion into our governance.

We must infuse compassion into our use of technology.

We must live in universal love for people of every religion and belief.

There are so many different practices and paths, but the core of bringing Heaven to Earth requires us to focus on maintaining simplicity and calmness.

Only in a state of equanimity can we acknowledge the multi-faceted needs of the whole and surrender to efforts needed to perpetually honor the process of maintaining harmony for all sentient beings. That degree of complexity is why it is best to simply think of the Divine and continue to serve with detached compassion.

Learn to inhabit buddha nature.

There is no barrier to enlightenment besides the walls within our minds.

Learn to be a buddha as you are.

In doing so, Earth will gradually come to reflect your inner state.

Release the conceptions blocking your buddhahood.

You are the Buddha of Light, Amitabha.

Slowly replace your thought realms with light realms through sadhana.

In the ultimate sense, there is no self behind all the identities at all, just spacious light.

By relating directly to this fundamental emptiness underlying all phenomena, we foster the light hidden in all things and all the aspects of life are automatically brought into harmony.

Your Divine embodiment is the final frontier for transforming Earth into Heaven.

Relate to your life simply and directly, but meditate each day until you ego dissolves into the universal state of empty luminosity.

Bask in it.

Whenever you are not in meditation, focus on shining forth brightly in all directions like the sun. The buddha nature living within you is incorruptible, like the brilliance of a diamond even while buried.

Each of our states of being effects the collective consciousness more than any of our rational minds can comprehend.

The greatest wisdom needed to achieve a heaven on our Earth is already within us all.

We must simply learn to let it emanate forth.

We must reach a point of engaging form with enough clarity that we reach beyond illusion.

Identification determines awareness, which creates the mandala-sphere we are inhabiting at any given moment.

Every attitude you maintain and action you bring forth are your offerings to the altar of now.

What you place on the altar of your attention is what you worship.

What you worship is given life and tends to grow.

If you wish to make the world more Divine in the here and now, make sure to put the Divine on the altar of your here and now.

This requires a lifestyle of meditation and promoting unity and harmony for billions of beings inhabiting the Earth.

If we serve total harmony, we will save humanity.

Although many paths of varying spiritual disciplines have been touched upon in this discourse, achieving the heights of heavenly repose is simpler than any phrase can ever reflect.

By turning within, you will find the transcendental bliss of the Divine.

By turning within, you will come to know God.

You don't necessarily need to go on group meditation retreats or learn intricate rituals.

You don't necessarily need to receive any initiations or to study many complicated scriptures.

You don't necessarily need to go on vast pilgrimages or achieve grand feats of austerity.

All that you need to bring Heaven to Earth is to rest attentively within as often and fully as possible.

All you need to bring Heaven to Earth is to meditate some each day.

Heaven is the everlasting joy hiding within you.

Heaven is a psychological state primarily and an external realm secondarily which is why there is such a tremendous importance to daily meditation.

As we come to normalize meditation so entirely that the essence of formlessness consciously becomes the most directive force of our species' mind stream, the Triadic Singularity will automatically emerge and the luminosity of an enlightened society will finally dawn for humanity.

Through spiritual self-effort we all come to embody our highest archetypes and then from such a state we will easily be able to establish an enlightened society.

Simply try to better the collective by bettering yourself.

This will bring the end to Earth as we have known it, a haven of suffering.

In turn, we will invoke the return of a utopia on Earth which could rightly be called Heaven.

ABOUT THE AUTHOR

Kevin Zeph (1990-present) is a devoted meditation practitioner and initiator, a spiritual advisor, a dharma artist (both visually and sonically), a keeper of the oracle of time, and an advocate for all global initiatives promoting peace. He has studied intensively with Sri Sri Sri Shivabalayogi Maharaj as well as with Mother Meera, Shri Anandi Ma and Sharon Jeffers. Kevin has worked closely with Bhagavan Das and many other profoundly wise elders over years and lifetimes.

To schedule a private consultation for guidance in meditation or to receive a oracle reading, please contact the author at:

kevinzeph.com

kevinzeph108@gmail.com

@kevrickzeph

Made in the USA
Columbia, SC
26 October 2021